OVERCOMING EXPLOITATION AND EXTERNALISATION

Advancing an intersectional theory of hegemony, this book shows how various power relations interact through capitalist structures of othering. Going beyond the usual critiques of capitalism, it analyses the market itself as a principal cause of various forms of externalisation and domination. The book therefore calls for a dismantling of the market and its competitive economic structures through a transformation of the economy from below, greater democratisation for the empowerment of suppressed identities, and the creation of commons as spaces based on inclusion rather than exclusion.

In doing so, *Overcoming Exploitation and Externalisation* argues that co-operative possibilities can emerge for the transformation of ourselves and our society. It will therefore appeal to scholars and students of social and political theory with interests in the commons and alternatives to capitalism.

Friederike Habermann is an independent economist, historian, and scholar-activist. Her research is particularly concerned with the inter-linkage of sexist, racist, classist, anthropocentric and other power relations with market society. She views commoning as a promising alternative to these power relations and she has been active as a press coordinator in the global grassroots movement, Peoples' Global Action.

CRITIQUES AND ALTERNATIVES TO CAPITALISM

Series editor: *Marcello Musto, Professor of Sociological Theory, York University, Canada*

This series publishes scholarly works on critiques and alternatives to capitalism, spanning a number of subject matters, political perspectives and geographical areas. It welcomes monographs and edited volumes in the fields of sociology, social and political theory and heterodox political economy, whose main areas of focus are the problems of capitalist society and its mode of production; alternatives to capitalism that address contemporary social issues; and 19th and 20th centuries anti-capitalist ideas and practical experiments.

Welcoming new perspectives on a wide range of themes, it seeks to explore alternative social-economic systems, critical theories of capitalism, social classes and inequality, public/private ownership and new contours of 'the commons', economic and financial crises, ecology, globalization, migration and citizenship, gender oppression, alienation, and cultural critique. The result is an eclectic, but focused and informative, series that provides original investigations, inspires significant conversations for today, and appeals to a diverse international audience.

Within and Beyond Capitalism
A Twofold Transformation
Dieter Klein

Overcoming Exploitation and Externalization
An Intersectional Theory of Hegemony and Transformation
Friederike Habermann

The Commons
A Force in the Socio-Ecological Transition to Postcapitalism
César Rendueles

For more information about this series, please visit: www.routledge.com/Critiques-and-Alternatives-to-Capitalism/book-series/CAATC

OVERCOMING EXPLOITATION AND EXTERNALISATION

An Intersectional Theory of Hegemony and Transformation

Friederike Habermann

Routledge
Taylor & Francis Group
LONDON AND NEW YORK

First published 2024
by Routledge
4 Park Square, Milton Park, Abingdon, Oxon OX14 4RN

and by Routledge
605 Third Avenue, New York, NY 10158

Routledge is an imprint of the Taylor & Francis Group, an informa business

British Library Cataloguing in Publication Data
A catalogue record for this book is available from the British Library

Library of Congress Cataloging-in-Publication Data
A catalog record has been requested for this book

ISBN: 978-1-032-44680-6 (hbk)
ISBN: 978-1-032-44681-3 (pbk)
ISBN: 978-1-003-37336-0 (ebk)

DOI: 10.4324/9781003373360

Typeset in Times New Roman
by Taylor & Francis Books

This book is dedicated to Silke Helfrich (1967–2021).

CONTENTS

ACKNOWLEDGEMENTS

Without Manfred Renken, this book would have got lost in translation. A huge gratitude for your commoning contribution!

Moreover, this book is the result of debates and shared experiences within countless spaces of other logics, shaped and sustained by unique beings I have been privileged to encounter in my life.

1

INTRODUCTION

"It's a saying you probably all know: that it's easier to imagine the end of the world than the end of capitalism", queer feminist philosopher Bini Adamczak begins in her opening speech at the so-called "conference of societalisation" in Berlin in autumn 2022. "However, today we no longer have to imagine the end of the world as we know it, because this end has already begun. It is in the news every day: in the form of poisoned rivers, over-acidified seas, burning forests, climate catastrophes galore, melting glaciers. But it also means that if we no longer have to use our inventiveness to imagine the end of the world, because we already have that in front of us, then we now have more time to imagine the end of capitalism." She continues: "We need to do so because the capitalist mode of production inevitably destroys this world of human and non-human animals."[1]

This is an assessment I share. Therefore this book analyses the causes of the devastation in the given, in particular how we got into it, thus opening our mind for ending capitalism towards a good life for all. Indeed, strictly speaking it is not only capitalism, but already the market economy as such that necessarily leads to manifold misery. In this, both the market and power relations along identity categories (such as racism and sexism) are interlinked. Herein the particular aspects can be understood as forms of exploitation and externalisation. Therefore, intersectional subject positions are of no less importance. A look at history shows how essential the safeguarding of privileges was (and is) in constructing the economy as we know it.

DOI: 10.4324/9781003373360-1

Such considerations reveal as well that structures are and have to be reproduced by subjects. Daily. This opens up emancipatory perspectives. Structures can neither be overcome by individual agency nor at once. But also no structure is ultimately fixed. Understanding how we got into this state of affairs makes it easier to find a way out. Against the background of existing practices of solidarity, the presented analysis aims at pointing out emerging paths towards an emancipatory society, in which exploitation and externalisation may never completely disappear, but will at least no longer be necessary components of social reproduction.

This means a fundamental change, even of a lot of everyday understandings so far taken for granted and unquestionable. This is probably the reason for a theoretical break that can often be found in transformation theories: The proposed solutions remain superficial and do not solve what was criticised in the analytical part. Conversely, there is a widespread idea, especially in social movements, of a radical break in the sense of a revolution that will change everything completely – without the necessary new modes of production and life being established in practices beforehand. In his book *This Life*, Martin Hägglund compares this to the religious hope for a paradise and advocates a "secular vision of why everything depends on what we do with our time together" (2019:27).

In this sense, this book looks back at the construction of the seemingly self-evident concepts of ownership, labour, exchange value and the interlinked identity categories for the purpose of describing ways of their deconstruction in the sense of an emancipatory reconstruction. The basic thesis behind this is: Even though othering can occur in any society, it is structurally embedded in the market society as externalisation. Therefore, othering cannot be overcome exclusively through unlearning. Neither can externalisation in the narrower economic sense nor exploitation in all its facets be resolved without overcoming the underlying hyperseparation, which divides the world, in a formulation by Val Plumwood (1993), into a kingdom of ends and a kingdom of means. And without, in Gayatri C. Spivak's (1996:4) words, "unlearning one's privileges as one's loss", there can be no democratic desire for a fundamental overcoming of exploitation and externalisation.

Jason W. Moore (2015) understands this hyperseparation as the splitting off of NATURE from SOCIETY: NATURE is that which is defined as a resource, available to SOCIETY for consumption. He places this Cartesian binarity at the centre of his analysis of the Capitalocene – the term he opposes to the Anthropocene as more appropriate. This binarity is created out of the dialectic of value formation as abstract societal labour and abstract societal nature. Together with Raj Patel, this connection is summarised in the plural as "frontiers": "Frontiers are frontiers because they are the encounter zones between capital and all kinds of nature – humans included. They are always, then, about reducing the costs of doing business. Capitalism not only *has* frontiers; it exists only *through* frontiers" (2017:18f).

Such frontiers also constitute the boundaries between identity categories. Generally speaking, their constructions have also emerged directly or indirectly interlinked with labour allocations. This serves capitalism, but also the privileged, whether it is to reduce the costs of doing business or to enjoy a pleasant division of labour. This does not exclude the importance of privileges that cannot be grasped in economic terms, such as access to another person's body without their clear consent. Instead of discussing identity politics and economic concerns against each other, we need to understand them as inextricably interlinked (Habermann 2008).

"Why can feminists have revolution now, while Marxists have to wait?", J. K. Gibson-Graham provoked in their book *The End of Capitalism* (1996:251). They question why, on the one hand, the image prevails that sexism is something we (re)construct in our everyday lives and can therefore change in our everyday actions and thus also bring about societal change – while, on the other hand, capitalism is understood as a totalitarian structure whose transformation takes place exclusively on the societal level, beyond personal behaviour. The answer is: Waiting to change the economy at some point is like waiting for Godot. In vain. But feminists can only believe in revolution in the here and now if they overlook the fact that the positions hitherto structurally occupied by women will merely be passed on in a classist and/or racist way as long as there is no abolition of the economic structure, which in turn is based on the hyperseparation between NATURE and SOCIETY.

Furthermore, this hyperseparation does not only (re)produce identity categories that are not self-determined and which serve not least to legitimise the assignment of unpleasant work, but also reproduces within ourselves, who in the given system are supposed to select our own parts according to usability. Overcoming all of these aspects would lead to a completely different way of life and economy.

The intersectional theory of hegemony is queer and materialist at once

But how can we achieve a very different way of living and re/production? Based on our experiences in the global resistance movement such as in Seattle in 1999 and as part of the worldwide networking of grassroots movements, *Peoples' Global Action*, in 2000 Raj Patel and I asked:

> If our interactive processes of construction and self-construction construct *sex* and *race*, is there – on the level of everyday knowledge and everyday action – also a *doing capitalism*? Construction of reality does not mean that it is constantly changing or changeable, but that reality, which appears to be stable, is not given, but is actively (re-)produced. Is capitalism also produced anew by us every day? But then it should also be possible to confront it que(e)r (German 'sich quer stellen' – defy the rules).
>
> *(Habermann/Patel 2000:19; cf 2000a)*

Later, using the term *Queeremos!* (in reference to *Venceremos! We will overcome!*), I have elaborated on the transformation of identities and the transformation of society (including the economy) as inextricably linked (Habermann 2009/2016). A change of society is unthinkable without a change of us as subjects, since both cannot be thought of separately. Just as it makes no sense to consider what we would have done in a past historical era – we simply would not be us. Conversely, any change in us will also change the societal and material context. The world shapes us, and we shape the world.

It is also in this sense that I have always understood both the Marxian legacy (though often not the Marxist one) and post-structuralist (and thus queer) theory (Habermann 2017). It was Marx himself who radically broke with theories based on either a purely essentialist or a purely determinist image of the human being. Marx writes in the Economical-Philosophical Manuscripts, "*just as* society itself produces *man as man*, so is society *produced* by him" (1844:44); and also in the first volume of *Capital*: "By thus acting on the external world and changing it, he at the same time changes his own nature" (1867:127). Marx examined all aspects of society, and thus also of the economy, as a relation, that is, as a relationship to one another. That Marx conceived of everything as a relation is the truly materialist movement of thought, argue Ernesto Laclau and Chantal Mouffe (1985:112). Indeed, to put it the other way round, this interweaving of people and society without one-sided determination is nothing else than the basic poststructuralist idea.

The intersectional hegemony theory presented in chapter 2 is not a new theory in the strict sense. Rather, such an intersectional theory emerges from the interplay of various existing approaches. It is based on Antonio Gramsci's (1933) theory of hegemony, which claims to include the diversity of power relations. In the words of Nicos Poulantzas (1977), the modern state becomes clear as a material condensation of power relations, which is something very different from a neutral image of democratic will formation. But Gramsci does not live up to his own claim, since all the privileges he considers remain reducible to class contradiction. Stuart Hall (1989) is to thank for the inclusion of racist privilege, and thus also sexist and others.

The dimension of externalisation constituting such a hegemonic historical bloc which represents modern western society is made visible through Spivak's analysis of the subaltern position: excluded both from privilege and from the discourse of civil society in which participation in privilege is struggled for. The answer to Spivak's famous question *Can the Subaltern Speak?* (1988) is an implicit "No": Subalterns do not have the power to make themselves heard. Regarding transformation, radical critique that stems from subaltern positions is either not noticed at all, or not understood but interpreted within the existing discursive framework, or dismissed as naïve, utopian, extremist, etc.

Like Spivak, but much more explicitly formulated in relation to hegemony theory, Laclau/Mouffe overcome the structuralist and thus ultimately essentialist premise of Gramsci's theory of hegemony. They emphasise that an articulation between elements modifies the preceding elements as a result, so that there are shifts of or production of interests and identities. This also means that just as every identity is contingently, i.e. not predeterminable, but due to structures also not accidently, related to its conditions of existence, every change in one identity entails changes in others.

Surprisingly, Laclau/Mouffe do not link their epistemology to racism and sexism. It is Judith Butler who focuses on the construction and changeability of subjects and overcomes the essentialist distinction between sex as a biological identity and gender as a social identity by showing that there is no sex that is not already gender, which means that there is no natural body that pre-exists its cultural inscription. Contrary to what she is often accused of, she does this without negating corporeality or materiality, and explicitly without understanding "nature" as a blank page, only shaped by discourse (Butler 1993). But I share the criticism often voiced that both matter and societal context remain underexposed in Butler's work. In this context, Bini Adamczak warns against ontologising the societal context as bad and thus assuming the inability to revolutionise relations ("die Unrevolutionierbarkeit der Verhältnisse"; 2017:236), which can then only be subversively undermined again and again.

Authors such as Donna Haraway, Karen Barad, Jason W. Moore and others not only focus on matter in prominent new ways, but also open up the theoretical space for the fact that our world consists of more than people and matter. Moore speaks of *oikeios* for the web of relations co-produced by the manifold configurations of "humanity-in-nature", of environments and organisms, of land, water, air, and life. Accordingly, agency is supposed to be a relational property of specific bundles of human and non-human nature. The Covid 19 pandemic became a striking example of this. But I have to admit that this claim is not redeemable for me at this point in the historical parts of the book.

The quintessence of what I call intersectional hegemony theory is that the struggle for hegemony does not only take place as an expression of the capitalist relationship, but tends to take place in all spheres of society and between all identity categories. In all of these contexts sex, race and class etc. are articulated categories; they always exist in relation to each other. But unlike sex, race and class etc. all and every individual is ultimately subjected to capitalism. While it is undisputed that the concentration of capital, especially in recent decades, has led to exorbitant differences in power, in the end, capitalism structures and limits the agency of all of us. Particularly this also applies to overall societal decisions of putting a stop to the crises.

Capitalism is nothing external to us. To borrow a term from Michel Foucault (1975): We form the correlate, i.e. the appropriate counterpart for these structures, with our identities. From this, one starting point of emancipatory politics might be transforming ourselves by de-identifying with our assigned subject positions, be they economic or gendered or whatever (by the way, for this we need others, otherwise we are not even capable of recognising our privileges as such). This does change the societal context already because it is based on us. But we need to focus on queering materialist conditions as well, because nevertheless they limit our capacity for change. This means, in general, to shift the structures that shape and enable us, of which a starting point can be to reject our identitarian invocation as economic and/or gendered etc. subjects. Whether this is in everyday shifts or in militant protests is up to political practice. In essense, all that is possible is necessary for transformation.

Assuming contingency instead of determinacy does not make it easy to free ourselves from structural constraints. We are bound to these structures by body and psyche, by direct and discursive threats of sanctions, and by economic constraints. However, since standstill is not possible due to the necessity of everyday reproductions which are never identically repeatable, our subjectivities and the structures embedding us are always in flux. But fundamental structures limit our agency. Changes will peter out or become the same in a new form if we do not manage to grasp the fundamental causes.

To illustrate: If we live in a house, the objects in it and especially the walls will limit and guide our actions, but not prescribe them in detail. In the course of our everyday reproduction, such as brushing our teeth or drinking coffee, the toothbrush or coffee cup will never be in exactly the same place – even if we tried. There will always be a slight change, the identical daily repetition (iteration) does not exist. Especially not in a changing world. And we might even put the cup somewhere else on purpose. Or change it. Or even a piece of furniture. Shifts often take place in our daily actions that make up our way of existence. But it is only through a collective effort that the walls, and thus the essential structure of the house, can be transformed.

But for this, in turn, an articulation is needed as a first step, in which the desire for change is given space to become intelligible, perceptible to ourselves. Such articulations can form "Räume anderer Selbstverständlichkeit" ["spaces of other logics"] (Habermann 2009) that can arise everywhere in our everyday life, fleeting or lasting. Here it could be decisive that queering material relations can also mean in a narrower sense tracking down and overcoming binaries in societal and not least economic logics. For example, when the opposition of a concept of property, which enables a few people to have as much as half of humanity, and which only makes ownership or possessionlessness visible as alternatives, is dissolved in commons, thus enabling a having that allows everyone to live well. Or when it comes to the fact that only those in labour relations are allowed to eat, and that in the binary understanding we all like to lie lazily in the hammock – while this kind of work is often harmful to the world, and this binarity prevents us from doing what is really important and/or truly fulfils us.

The more comprehensive these spaces of other logics are, the more significant they may be for transformation. But within capitalism and all kinds of power relations, they will necessarily remain incomplete, and yet even these incomplete spaces of other logics allow subjects to develop differently than within the pure hegemonic system. Without these incomplete spaces that allow for other logics and new subjectivites, it is unlikely that a hegemonic turn will be achieved.

Exploitation and externalisation

For an approach that focuses on *Overcoming Exploitation and Externalisation*, it may at first seem paradoxical that theories which see an outside as a prerequisite for every identity serve as a theoretical basis. After all, the (post-)structuralist basic assumption is that an identity can only be formed on the basis of exclusion and thus a process of externalisation. Even a completely emancipatory society would have all non-emancipatory forms of society as an outside. What makes the difference can be captured with self-determination and care. Subjects in a compulsory heterosexual society are only allowed to conform to certain identities and to love certain other identities. In an achieving society we have to perform and suppress most aspects of our being. In a truly needs-oriented society, however, all subjects can live and articulate themselves according to their contingent being. While having to remain in predetermined structures and identities is domination, domination, whether personal or structural, is "power-over", queering is "power-to". What makes up this queer desire? It is the striving for, with Michel Foucault: the art of not being governed in this way, with Bini Adamczak: of not being identified in this way, with Jason Moore: of not having to live in this way. But only "power-with" as a co-active-form achieves an emancipatory change of structures that (staying with the image of the house) does not let us run into a wall, but opens new spaces that alter the rest of the house, and make new subjectivities possible in a sustainable way. This cannot happen individually. The striving for an emancipatory society not only requires collectivity, it is in itself a desire that carries collectivity. It includes the overcoming of exploitation and externalisation to the utmost extent.

Domination always represents both exploitation and externalisation, because every domination can only be constituted in a certain identity category. Only through identity frontiers can it be determined who has privileges and who does not. Who receives resources and who does not. Who is allowed to do nothing or at least choose activities and who is not. Any hegemony co-constructs identity. Externalisation happens, is produced and also made through separation, through othering, through making invisible or placing in the shadow. What and who is inside and what and who is outside depends on the hegemonic power relations, interlinked with the regime of accumulation. What is inside and what is outside, that is, what men are, what women are, what panda bears are and what cattle for slaughter are, always remains a contingent result. Chapter 3 shows how we got to where we are now.

At the same time, we all live under one rule that does not need a privileged subject, that even ultimately subjugates all subjects: It is by the law of value that even "rulers" are "being governed in this way", that their performance, to use a Butlerian expression, has to conform to very specific guidelines. A top manager who tries to evade this will very quickly lose their share and/or position and be replaced by a competitor. The law of value, which seeks to reduce all of nature to something exchangeable, including human beings, stops at nothing and no one.

However, no human nor non-human living creature wants to be reduced to something interchangeable, as Moore puts it. At a certain point, all life rebels against the value-monoculture nexus of modernity; no human being, no living being, wants to do the same thing day in and day out (2015:315). Ultimately all life resists purely functional utilisation for accumulation (Saave 2022:20).

The law of value is not a metahistorical force, but it is virulent in the current drama of climate and other crises. Gopal Dayaneni illustrates this with a scene from the 1977 film *Star Wars*, which at the same time makes it clear that we are not currently dealing with a house (as I have illustrated it above), but with a trash compactor: The heroes have got into one. The walls of the compressor are coming closer and closer. In this picture, the walls are the crises, but the moving force behind them is the market, or more precisely, the law of value, which arises out of the market, and at the same time forms the driving force of the market. At first, the problem for those in the centre seemed to be only the forced migration of others from the margins. But in the end, those in the centre have merely bought themselves time. In the film, the heroes try to stop the walls with a big metal bar – but this machine is there to destroy metal, and it cannot be stopped by the same means. In the same way, Dayaneni argues, market solutions fail trying to fight what the market has unleashed (2009:80).

The market – not only capitalism, mind you – stands in the way of a good life for all. It leads to the exclusion of many people from sufficient resources, because resources go where the money is, not where the need is. Moreover, artificial scarcity is required, because without unsatisfied demand, no equilibrium price can be formed. The market puts us under pressure to exploit ourselves since both our prosperity and also our societal recognition depends on professional success. This creates performance anxiety. And it produces what I call structural hatred: because if I get the job, everyone else does not get it. The market forces us, because we need money, to do things we do not want to do, and if we really like doing something, it is under circumstances we cannot choose freely. The market can only avoid economic and financial crises by growing and growing, but every growth also further exploits our planet. The market forces companies to use as many resources of nature, animals and humans as cheaply, i.e. underpaid or even unpaid, as possible, in order to be able to compete. The market puts the services of the Global South and caring activities at a disadvantage because of fewer opportunities for streamlining. In short, it imposes dynamics on us that most of us reject. And they lead us to disaster.

All these market effects, explained in chapter 4, can also be understood as exploitation and externalisation. To speak of exploitation and externalisation focuses on the necessarily constant coexistence inherent in the market economy of what is generally recognised as being part of the economy and its subjects as well as that which does not and yet flows into it. Externalised is the latter, exploited are both. In business and economics, externalities or external costs depict the passing on of costs to the community or to future generations. In psychology, externalisation describes the displacement of feelings, motivations or attributions to the exterior. The focus on externalisation thus allows us to look at both extracted economic spheres, and segregations in our identities, including those that are used to maintain identity categories.

All these aspects are closely related. Economic man as the subject of economic theory does not only represent the stereotype of the white male bourgeois, but both emerged in interaction. Women/people of colour and – as Michel Foucault has shown – lunatics and other identity categories emerged in distinction to him. None of these identities existed before as we know them today: Constructed as the excluded from the identity of the white heterosexual bourgeois male – as "the Other" – they either first developed as categories or underwent a fundamental shift in meaning.

In the meantime, economic man has become the overall role model, the guiding principle for (almost) all identities. Despite all the emancipation successes that have been achieved from anti-racist, anti-sexist and also anti-classist struggles in the meantime, these economic and identity concepts continue to be of decisive importance for how we experience our lives and how we can shape them. Processes in which people are de-gendered and de-raced in the sense that their hegemonic characteristics, being useful for a career, predominate, are parallel to those in which people from the social underclass rise: It is possible, but still more difficult due to positional disadvantages. Therefore it remains easier for those with the most hegemonic characteristic to succeed. This does not mean that all white male cis able-bodied, not underclass people etc. are always the winners. Rather, economic man is understood as an expression of a governmentality that has emerged between various relations of domination, prescribing patterns of behavior that favour some identities but ultimately subjugates all.

Just as we speak of economic man and his other, we can also speak of the monetary sphere – or in short: gross domestic income – and its other. In the German-speaking world, the term externalisation gained importance in the feminist-economic debate, not least through Adelheid Biesecker and Uta von Winterfeld (2014; 2023). It became more widely known with Stephan Lessenich's book *Living Well at Other's Expense* (2016), whose original German subtitle translates to *The externalisation society and its price.* A very comprehensive account was published in 2022 by Anna Saave: *Einverleiben und Externalisieren. Zur Innen-Außen-Beziehung der kapitalistischen Produktionsweise* [Incorporating and Externalising. On the Inside-Outside Relationship of the Capitalist Mode of Production].

The underlying analysis is epitomised through an iceberg model, originally designed by Maria Mies in 1979 for a lecture, which illustrates the economy including its hidden aspects (Bennholdt-Thomsen/Mies 1997:38). The upper, visible part of this iceberg represents the part generally considered to be the economy, i.e. the monetary sphere, and thus everything that is transacted via prices. This also includes wages. From Karl Marx we learnt how surplus value is siphoned off from workers because their costs of reproduction, reflected in wages, are lower for capital than what they add to the value of the products. This is what he calls exploitation. The part below the surface symbolises what is essential to the capitalist production process as externalised: the so-called ecosystem services as well as unpaid or underpaid activities, be it reproductive work in the household or subsistence activities (the latter not only, but especially in the Global

South). In the 1980s, the ecofeminists Maria Mies, Veronika Bennholdt-Thomsen and Claudia von Werlhof, known in Germany to this day as "die Bielefelderinnen" (the Bielefeld women), called this the triad of "women, nature and colonies" (Mies 1986). In both areas there is economic activity – in the "underwater area" (Anna Saave) in the sense of satisfying needs as the production of or for life, in the upper area valorisation as commodities, for the purpose of maximising profit. The underwater area subsidises the tip of the iceberg and is naturalised for this. Also all costs that capital does not want to pay are externalised into this sphere.

The joint major work of the Bielefeld women is called *Frauen, die letzte Kolonie* [Women, the Last Colony, 1983], since the form of appropriation is understood as analogous to robbery in the colonies. They see the "housewifisation" as decisive for this process. For this, activities such as housework are considered as a kind of leisure time activity and are not paid a living wage. This is not only in the interest of the capitalists, but it is also about the appropriation of female labour by men with housewives. The appropriation of racist advantages by whites is constantly set in parallel. However, ecofeminism, which in the word defines one relation of domination as the core, is accused of lacking intersectionality.[2]

The fundamental analysis behind the iceberg model is much older. In *Die Akkumulation des Kapitals [Accumulation of Capital]* (1913), Rosa Luxemburg showed that capitalism has always needed and will always need a supply of raw materials, labour and markets from outside. At that time, these came largely from the colonies, today, in addition to the postcolonial power structures that still exist, the market mechanism would be sufficient. The same is true for the undervaluation of care work.

The existence of postcolonial and patriarchal power structures is undisputed. Furthermore, the logics of the market cannot be separated from postcolonial and patriarchal power-knowledge complexes. However, even if it may seem so in the historical perspective, since all too often even scientific knowledge perfectly served hegemonic interests, this must not be imagined as conspiracy. As a rule, it is the result of discourses that were mostly determined by hegemonic interest groups that did not even recognise themselves as such, but rather mutually assured each other of the naturalness and correctness of their own privileges and thus in turn shaped reality.

This gave rise to economic relations and a common sense based on seemingly given concepts as e.g. the modern concept of ownership (in German this modern understanding is called *Eigentum* and legally distinguished from *Besitz*, which is translated as "possession") on the one hand and on the other hand affiliations to identity groups.[3] Racist, sexist etc. identity categories as well as the entire separation of NATURE from SOCIETY arose in the course of capitalist development and is therefore immanent to it.

To speak of exploitation and externalisation is one possible approach, not the only one. David Harvey's expression of "Accumulation by Dispossession" for the ongoing, and in his view no longer "primitive" accumulation received much attention. He states that capitalism is dependent on an outside, and also adds that this is not simply found, but "capitalism necessarily and always creates its own other" (Harvey 2003:141). Instead of a linear process, it is a matter of waves of valuation and devaluation. The classic example of this is the industrial reserve army, as Marx already named it. Klaus Dörre, who operates with the German term "Landnahme" [land grabbing], gives the example of a fitter who is dismissed as a permanent employee and then re-employed as a subcontractor (Dörre 2013:100f). For Harvey, this would be a typical process of devaluation, "by which capitalism creates its own other" (2013:151).

The idea of creating the exterior is also inherent in the concept of housewifisation (Saave 2022:81). Through neoliberalism, the reserve army of housewifes in the Global North has meanwhile been largely included again as a labour force. But can such processes really be turned back and forth? Resistance would also have to be taken into account here, stemming from the alteration of identities and interests of the concerned subjects, having made new experiences, having developed new desires. Moreover, Rosa Luxemburg pointed out that exclusive access to workers who had already been discarded once was not sufficient for capital's sudden expansion needs (1913:283). And the primitive accumulation as the (ongoing) loss of the possibility of subsistence or, in Marx's formulation, the means of production, is overwhelmingly a chain of one-off events. Moore emphasises the historical uniqueness of each of these occasions. This is all the more true in the case of natural resources. In the words of Nicholas Georgescu-Roegen (1971), they are irreversibly degraded when put to use in economic activity. As with conventional recycling, these are generally no longer resources of equal value. At the same time, Moore also understands NATURE as not simply found, but actively co-produced, made possible by a mix of economy, science, power and culture.

Another aspect for not adhering to Harvey's terminology lies in his understanding of accumulation by dispossession as a crisis-solving strategy for capitalism and therefore becoming dominant in neoliberalism as a

New Imperialism (2003) rather than inherent in the market mechanism itself. Isabel Feichtner and Geoff Gordon, speaking of exploitation and extraction in *Constitutions of Value* call "into question the diagnosis that contemporary crises are prompted by a decoupling of value from values, and allows us to understand the current state not as a deterioration of a desirable status quo" (2023:10). They emphasise that the history of colonialism reveals how professing liberal values coincides with establishing capitalist value practices at the cost of displacing alternative economies and ways of life, and how these values enable and sustain such value practices. Accordingly, it is central for any project invested in change to focus on both kinds of value practices.

Beatrice Müller's (2016) value-abstraction approach also takes these two levels into consideration. The permanent outsourcing and devaluation of care (work) in capitalism is, on the one hand, due to the competitive production, i.e. incorporated unpaid and thus externalised for economic reasons. This is true even in paid relations, among other things by making relational elements invisible. For this, Müller largely endorses Roswitha Scholz's (2005) value dissociation theorem. On the other hand, this devaluation and dissociation also corresponds to the "abjection" on the cultural-symbolic level identified by the French psychoanalyst Julia Kristeva (1980), i.e. dismissal of what is not provided for in the symbolic order. Beyond this, Müller deviates from Kristeva's adoption of the universalist theorisations by Freud and Lacan and refers to Judith Butler's reading according to which the process of abjection and the object of abjection have the same ontological status, i.e. the latter is not to be thought of as pre-social, but as the outside threatening the subject (and ultimately the stability of society). Similar to the value dissociation theorem by Scholz, Moore (2015:39) speaks of the dialectic of appropriation and capitalisation. This is controlled by a logic of value accumulation that reduces the world to zones of exploitation according to surplus value, and zones of direct appropriation. "Appropriation" is seen as a productive activity, no less than "exploitation". And yet, this remains a massive blind spot in radical thinking. For Moore, this is not least reflected in the overlooking of indigenous people being forced to work for the colonisers as the great revolution of labour productivity representing the beginning of capitalism.

Finally I want to mention the recent book by Nancy Fraser, *Cannibal Capitalism* (2022). Fraser speaks of the division into the "capitalist realm" and the "natural realm", about the distinction between a historical humanity and an ahistorical nature, and of "the front story of exploitation and the back story of expropriation" (2022:8/11), abbreviating this as "ex and ex". She examines the areas of ecological, racist and care "ex and ex" contexts separately and looks for possibilities of a socialist overcoming. However, for her, commons are merely small niches that have neither much protest nor transformation potential. In chapter 5, when I present the three paths of transformation that also the Network Economic Transformation (NOW NET) stands for, it will become clear that from a commoning perspective and Fraser's aspiration to strive for radical democracy assumed, Fraser's concept would also amount to a commons society. In this respect, Fraser's approach is both a prominent analysis of capitalism as a whole, which, by the way, is probably based far more on the approaches already presented here than is made clear in the book, and a typical example of how proposed solutions cannot live up to the analysis, since some (race, gender, the externalisation of reproduction from production etc.) but not everything (property, labour, market) is recognised as first constructed and then naturalised.

To imagine transformation

As deeply as the processes analysed here are rooted in the materialist and scientific revolutions since the early modern times, transformation requires correspondingly profound upheavals at all levels. Yet economics remains crucial. Just as hyperseparation emerged together with the market, dismantling the market by pushing back the principle of competition and thus the functional mode of the market forms one central path. This can take many forms.

When as a consequence decisions are no longer made by the market, from an emancipatory perspective these must not be taken over by a central power, be it a dictator or a central state. This results in a by necessity comprehensive democratisation of society as the second path to transformation. Whereby more democracy does not mean being allowed to vote more often, but more real participation in the shaping of one's own and common life-world.

This in turn gives rise to the third way: When people begin to organise their lives in an increasingly democratic way, they begin to create commons. Commons or commoning means taking care in common of the needs of life, and/or re/producing them. This has nothing to do with organising this in a small way – on the contrary, commoning makes frontiers, where not dissolved, permeable. Patterns of commoning can be applied at every level.

There is justified criticism of the concept of democracy, not least because the societies that adorn themselves with it have always been based on exclusion and externalisation. In his book *Grenzen der Demokratie* [Limits of Democracy] (2019), the externalisation theorist Lessenich also reminds us that if the democratic space is limited to the privileged, privileges are not overcome. This insight also goes back to Luxemburg who learned it the hard way. In 1913 she published *Die Akkumulation des Kapitals*, though as she wrote, from time to time she was oppressed by the thought that all theoretically interested followers of Marx's doctrine would declare for granted her findings, explained and justified in such detail, to be a matter of course. "Things turned out differently." At the time, the reaction to her book from the German left was an unanimous condemnation. "As far as I can remember, such a fate has never been accorded to a new publication of party literature, since it has existed, and it is really not all gold and pearls", she wrote, and concluded: "The unusual nature of all these events clearly reveals that other passions than 'pure science' have probably been touched by the book in one way or another" (1915/1966:238f).

This assumption still suggests itself more than a hundred years later. This very point Stephan Lessenich calls the life lie of the settled left in capitalism: the "unwillingness to know" that the relative prosperity of Western lower classes is also based on a structural exploitation of the Global South. Structural externalisation allows for this power to be ignorant ("Macht zur Unwissenheit") as a collective attitude, thus also making possible the resulting ignorant ways of acting as, in the terminology of Ulrich Brand and Markus Wissen, *The Imperial Mode of Living* (2017). Conversely, this ignorance stabilises the hegemony of the existing relations of exploitation and externalisation in all their complexity.

We allow ourselves to be exploited and exploit others because competition or the logic of exchange compels us to do so. But when it comes to our own privileges, it is often also because we can do it. No one likes to be confronted with how we defend our privileges. Therefore, it should be emphasised once again: The dismantling of subaltern positions can only be carried out democratically and economically if, at the same time, the "unlearning of one's privileges as one's loss" makes democratic desire possible in the first place, at least among a critical mass of subjects.

Moreover, we allow ourselves to be exploited and we exploit others because we have forgotten to see how differently we could live. This is what Marx calls fetishism. Here too, as with the subaltern position for overcoming the hegemonic common sense and as with unlearning privilege, common political practice is essential for new horizons of thought and action. Accordingly, the solution-oriented part of this book is essentially based on current insights of transformational movements.

Reflections on an emancipatory future are always possible only to a limited extent. This is where theory and practice come together directly. Only in the process of queering both subjects and societal context (as subcultural spaces of other logics or as mainstream) can common sense be transcended and, in the long run, the fetishised economic manifestations as well as the identities interdependent in them radically transformed. At present, commons and commoning are crystallising as essential for this. The Parisian legal anthropologist Étienne Le Roy describes the coming into motion through experiences of commoning:

> As soon as the first domino falls over – by invoking the commons – many of the concepts on which the idea of modern Western civilization rest lose their apparent balance, and the whole edifice, previously believed to be well-founded, collapses onto itself: the state, the law, the market, the nation, work, contracts, debts, giving, the juristic person, private property, as well as institutions such as kinship, marital law, and the law of succession, are suddenly called into question.
>
> *(Le Roy 2015:277)*

Notes

1 Vergesellschaftungskonferenz Eröffnungspanel: Bini Adamczak https://www.youtube.com/watch?v=jKme9Cf_4zE (15.06.2023; translation F. H. Hereafter English citations in the text are sometimes the author's translations of the German original. Please refer to the References section in each instance.)

2 Is Ecofeminism still relevant? Channel Our Changing Climate; https://www.youtube.com/watch?v=VBP0-XUe6bU (15.06.2023).

3 This happened out of a Europe that was trying to make the rest of the world a colony. Therefore, the representation of these developments will be a Eurocentric one (without wanting to deny a bias due to my own location in Germany).

References

Adamczak, Bini (2017) *Beziehungsweise Revolution. 1917, 1968 und kommende*, Frankfurt/M.: Suhrkamp.

Bennholdt-Thomsen, Veronika/Mies, Maria (1997) *Eine Kuh für Hillary. Die Subsistenzperspektive*, Munich: Frauenoffensive.

Bennholdt-Thomsen, Veronika/Mies, Maria/Werlhof, Claudia von (1983) *Frauen, die letzte Kolonie. Zur Hausfrauisierung der Arbeit*, Reinbeck bei Hamburg: Rowohlt.

Biesecker, Adelheid/Winterfeld, Uta von (2014) "Extern? Weshalb und inwiefern moderne Gesellschaften Externalisierung brauchen und erzeugen", Working Paper 2, DFG-Kolleg Postwachstumsgesellschaften, Jena.

Biesecker, Adelheid/Winterfeld, Uta von (2023) *Wert ohne Herrschaft? Externalisierung als Prinzip kapitalistischer Wertbildung, Coronakrise und transformatorische Praxis*, mit Beiträgen von Andrea Baier und Andrea Vetter, Berlin/Toronto: Barbara Budrich Verlag.

Brand, Ulrich/Wissen, Markus (2017) *The Imperial Mode of Living. Everyday Life and the Ecological Crisis of Capitalism*, London/New York: Verso, 2021.

Butler, Judith (1993) *Bodies that Matter. On the Discursive Limits of Sex*, London/New York: Routledge.

Dayaneni, Gopal (2009) "Climate Justice in the US", in: *Critical Currents.* Dag Hammarskjöld Foundation Occasional Paper Series, No. 6, *Contours of Climate Justice. Ideas for Shaping New Climate and Energy Politics*, edited by Ulrich Brand/Nicola Bullard/Edgardo Lander/Tadzio Mueller, 80–84.

Dörre, Klaus (2013) "Landnahme und die Grenzen sozialer Reproduktion. Zur gesellschaftstheoretischen Bedeutung Rosa Luxemburgs", in: Ingo Schmidt (ed.), *Rosa Luxemburgs 'Akkumulation des Kapitals'. Die Aktualität von ökonomischer Theorie, Imperialismuserklärung und Klassenanalyse*, Hamburg: VSA Verlag, 82–116.

Feichtner, Isabel/Gordon, Geoff (eds.) (2023) *Constitutions of Value. Law, Governance, and Economic Value*, New York: Routledge.

Foucault, Michel (1975) *Discipline & Punish. The Birth of the Prison*, New York: Vintage Books.

Fraser, Nancy (2022) *Cannibal Capitalism. How Our System Is Devouring Democracy, Care, and the Planet – and What We Can Do about it*, London/New York: Verso.

Georgescu-Roegen, Nicolas (1971) *The Entropy Law and the Economic Process*, Cambridge, Massachusetts: Harvard University Press, 2014.

Gramsci, Antonio (1933) *Prison Notebooks* (Vols 1–3), edited by Antonio Callari, New York: Columbia University Press, 2011.

Habermann, Friederike (2017) "Nicht nur Identität, sondern auch materielle Verhältnisse queeren. Oder: Warum Marx und Butler dasselbe wollen", in: Christine Löw et al. (eds.), *Material Turn: Feministische Perspektiven auf Materialität und Materialismus*, Opladen: Budrich, 187–201.

Habermann, Friederike (2008) *Der homo oeconomicus und das Andere. Hegemonie, Emanzipation und Identität*, Baden-Baden: Nomos.

Habermann, Friederike (2009) *Halbinseln gegen den Strom. Anders leben und wirtschaften im Alltag*, Königstein: Ulrike Helmer-Verlag.

Habermann, Friederike (2016) *Ecommony. UmCARE zum Miteinander*, Sulzbach: Ulrike Helmer-Verlag.

Habermann, Friederike/Patel, Raj (2000) "Identitäten, hört die Signale! Sex, Race and WTO", in: *Jungle World-Dossier* No.1, 08.03.2000, 17–20; http://www.no-racism.net/s26/gender/identitaeten.htm (15.6.2023).

Habermann, Friederike/Patel, Raj (2000a) "Nach Seattle: Mit Queering gegen die WTO", in: *femina politica. Zeitschrift für feministische Politikwissenschaft*, 9. Jg, Heft *Feministische Ansätze in den internationalen Beziehungen* 1/2000, Berlin, 110–113.

Hägglund, Martin (2019) *This Life. Why Mortality Makes us Free*, London: Profile Books2020.

Hall, Stuart (1989–) *Ausgewählte Schriften* (Vols 1–3), Hamburg(/Berlin): Argument.

Harvey, David (2003) *The New Imperialism*, Oxford: Oxford University Press.

Kristeva, Julia (1980) *Powers of Horror. An Essay on Abjection*, New York: Columbia University Press, 1982.

Laclau, Ernesto/Mouffe, Chantal (1985) *Hegemony and Socialist Strategy. Towards a Radical Democratic Politics*; translated into German as *Hegemonie und radikale Demokratie. Zur Dekonstruktion des Marxismus*, Vienna, 2000.

Le Roy, Étienne (2015) "How I Have Been Conducting Research on the Commons for Thirty Years Without Knowing It", in: David Bollier/Silke Helfrich (eds.), *Patterns of Commoning*, Amherst: Off the Common Books.

Lessenich, Stephan (2016) *Neben uns die Sintflut. Die Externalisierungsgesellschaft und ihr Preis*, Berlin: Carl Hanser Verlag. Translated as *Living Well at Other's Expense. The Hidden Costs of Western Prosperity*, Medford: Polity Press, 2019.

Lessenich, Stephan (2019) *Grenzen der Demokratie. Teilhabe als Verteilungsproblem*, Stuttgart: Reclam.

Luxemburg, Rosa (1913) *Die Akkumulation des Kapitals. Ein Beitrag zur ökonomischen Erklärung des Imperialismus*, in: *Archiv sozialistischer Literatur 1*, Frankfurt: Verlag Neue Kritik, 1966, 1–380.

Luxemburg, Rosa (1915) "Was die Epigonen aus der Marxschen Theorie gemacht haben. Eine Antikritik", in: *Archiv sozialistischer Literatur 1*, Frankfurt: Verlag Neue Kritik, 1966, 381–482.

Marx, Karl (1844) *Economic & Philosophic Manuscripts of 1844*; https://www.marxists.org/archive/marx/works/download/pdf/Economic-Philosophic-Manuscripts-1844.pdf, 44.

Marx, Karl (1867) *Capital. A Critique of Political Economy*, Vol. I.; https://www.marxists.org/archive/marx/works/download/pdf/Capital-Volume-I.pdf.

Mies, Maria (1986) *Patriarchy and Accumulation on a World Scale*, London: Zed Books.

Moore, Jason W. (2015) *Capitalism in the Web of Life. Ecology and the Accumulation of Capital*, London/New York: Verso; translated into German as *Kapitalismus im Lebensnetz. Ökologie und die Akkumulation des Kapitals*, Berlin: Matthes & Seitz, 2020.

Müller, Beatrice (2016) *Wert-Abjektion. Abwertung von Care-Arbeit im patriarchalen Kapitalismus am Beispiel der ambulanten Pflege*, Münster: Westfälisches Dampfboot.

Patel, Raj/Moore, Jason W. (2017) *A History of the World in Seven Cheap Things. A Guide to Capitalism, Nature, and the Future of the Planet*, Oakland: University of California Press.

Plumwood, Val (1993) *Feminism and the Mastery of Nature*, London/New York: Routledge, 2003.

Poulantzas, Nicos (1977) *State, Power, Socialism*, London/New York: New Left Books, 1978.

Saave, Anna (2022) *Einverleiben und Externalisieren. Zur Innen-Außen-Beziehung der kapitalistischen Produktionsweise*, Bielefeld: transcript.

Scholz, Roswitha (2005) *Differenzen der Krise – Krise der Differenzen. Die neue Gesellschaftskritik im globalen Zeitalter und der Zusammenhang von 'Rasse', Klasse, Geschlecht und postmoderner Individualisierung*, Bad Honnef: Horlemann.

Spivak, Gayatri Chakravorty (1988) "Can the Subaltern Speak?", in: Patrick Williams/Laura Chrisman (eds.), *Colonial Discourse and Post-Colonial Theory. A Reader*, New York: Columbia University Press, 1994, 66–111.

Spivak, Gayatri Chakravorty (1996). *The Spivak Reader*. Edited by Donna Landry/Gerald Maclean, New York/London: Routledge.

2

INTERSECTIONAL THEORY OF HEGEMONY

In order to get to the bottom of the interlinkage of capitalism with sexism, racism and other power relations (including classism) and to trace possibilities for their abolition, a tool is needed that can both grasp the power structures in their multiplicity and is open to interactions. Antonio Gramsci's concept of hegemony provides a suitable basis for this.

In the following, I will start from this and show how a Marxist and an intersectional analysis can be combined in a non-essentialist way. As already mentioned, intersectional hegemony theory is anything but a genuinely designed theory. The fact that so little attention is paid to how well approaches that are often discussed in contradictory ways fit together, is surely also due to the fact that we have different aspects in mind when we refer to a theorist and their ideas. Related to this is the finding that in the secondary literature there are sometimes severe distortions of the original statements. Thirty years ago, Judith Butler called *For a careful reading* (1995) – not successfully, as numerous later examples of reception show. These are two reasons why I am tracing the thoughts of various theorists from scratch in the following. The third reason lies in the effort to write in such a way that people without prior knowledge can also understand the argumentation.

In his prison notes, Antonio Gramsci (who, as leader of the Italian Communist Party, was imprisoned under fascism under Benito Mussolini in 1926) significantly explores the question of why attempts at

DOI: 10.4324/9781003373360-2

revolution in Western Europe failed (Gramsci 1929–33). What made these societies so stable? On the contrary, historical materialism had predicted that a bourgeois revolution would have to precede a socialist revolution. Gramsci's answer: In bourgeois societies, instead of only a few profiteers on one side and many exclusively exploited on the other, there is a complex structure with different distributions of privileges.

He thus understands hegemony not as domination based exclusively on coercion, but as the leadership of a class that attempts to establish a societal consensus in order to secure its hegemonic position in this way. This is not a consensus negotiated in the emancipatory sense. The rulers must succeed in binding as many people as possible to themselves who are not directly involved in the rule by constructing commonalities with them. According to Gramsci, pure ideology will not suffice for this. In bourgeois societies, quite far-reaching concessions are made, which stabilises them. But beyond that, hegemony exerts an intellectual-ideological dominance and attraction effect. Even groups whose interests contradict the hegemonic group are discursively drawn into its ideological maelstrom which is thus largely reproduced by them – in a consensual way, as it seems – in everyday life (Gramsci 1929–33:1947).

Gramsci criticises the lack of a clear representation of the state in Marxist theory. Here he makes a distinction. By "political society" Gramsci understands the state in the narrower sense, which rules through force, by "civil society" those institutions and organisations which encompass the social activities of the people, i.e. the political, intellectual, cultural and moral leadership in society as a whole. Hegemony is supported in and by civil society. This is where the struggle for hegemony, i.e. the political, intellectual, cultural and moral leadership in society as a whole, takes place, since only here can democratic processes and emancipatory movements emerge. Domination, i.e. foregoing a consensual element, is only exercised upon those who are excluded from political society and civil society.

If a class proves to be capable of leadership, i.e. if its hegemonic position is based on consent and consensus on the part of those to whom it extends, then according to Gramsci we can speak of a historical bloc. A historical bloc is thus the alliance of certain social and political forces, of rulers and ruled, with a certain common sense, rooted in the real societal structures, especially the relations of production. A new historical bloc always means a change in these elements.

The prerequisites for the transformation of a society look accordingly. Gramsci speaks of a "war of position" in contrast to a "war of movement". In earlier revolutions, the aim was to eliminate oppressive conditions through a show of force, limited in time and space, that was to culminate in the assumption of state power – e.g., the storming of the Bastille in the French Revolution in 1789 or in Russia in 1917. Gramsci calls this approach "movement war". He sees this as no longer possible in bourgeois societies, since power is not only secured institutionally and militarily in the state apparatus, but is based on hegemony. Instead, the state and society would have to be transformed from within in a revolutionary way. This is what Gramsci calls a "war of position". The battle for hegemony in civil society is therefore at the forefront of the war of position.

Gramsci coined the term Fordism and essentially applied the theory of hegemony to this societal formation that was forming in his time. The Ford factory represents the historical turn where workers earned so much they were enabled to buy their own products. Therefore there was an interest for the capitalist class to maintain a relatively high wage to allow for sales. For their part, many workers were happy to settle into this life. The extremely monotonous and intensive, therefore physically and mentally exhausting forms of work were seen as societally unquestionable. The result was a class compromise in which the workers' struggle has nothing to do with transformation efforts, but revolves around working conditions and, not least, wage levels.

Graphically, such a historical bloc can be illustrated as a block, as a square. In Gramsci's formulation, the ruling classes are at the top, together with the state institutions in the narrower sense. This passes into civil society as a state in the broader sense, which is the much larger part. It is here where the struggle for hegemony takes place, not least by trade unions and other forces for shares of privileges or the surplus value.

How sharply the transitions between the rulers and the ruled is depicted depends on how sharply or smoothly this transitions into highlypaid managerial floors, later into a well-paid skilled worker class, all the way to the low-wage sector, the long-term unemployed, the homeless.

Several considerations are relevant here. Top manager salaries can run into the millions these days, but individual owners of companies have tens of billions at their disposal. So is class decisive? Shareholder value and thus shares in added value can, however, also be acquired from an employee position, and conversely, many small entrepreneurs with only a few employees do not have the money for this, as they can hardly make ends meet in the competitive struggle, and the financial market naturally harbours many risks. Is the border then, according to pure wealth, between the often-named 1 per cent and the 99 per cent? Or, from a post-colonial point of view, are the interests – as long as relative poverty within the historical bloc represents relative wealth at the expense of what is externalised, today including the "slow violence" (Rob Nixon 2011) – shifted into the future?

Visualised in this way as a square, and assuming that among the non-ruling classes different groups can achieve very different concessions for themselves, the spatial location from top to bottom and thus in the hierarchy of this historical bloc shows the distribution of privileges.

The location in the square also shows the possibilities of societal influence. Decisive for the civil society struggle of the different forces for concessions or even hegemony is the societal power a group can activate in the sense of potentially challenging the prevailing order. Or, conversely, visible becomes the proximity between certain groups and the instruments of power of the narrower state, relevant to asserting the own interests against groups that have a less "strong arm".

The struggle for inclusion

In this attempt at visualisation, today's intersectional discourses easily slip into the picture. But slowly: neither women nor the societal position of women appear in Gramsci's analysis of Fordism. This is surprising from today's perspective, since Gramsci focuses precisely on the interplay of different power relations, and his goal is a society in which no social group occupies a subordinated position. But since for him hegemony originates in the factory (Gramsci 1929–33:2069), Gramsci ultimately does not include other power relations in his analysis. His emphasis on the autonomy of civil society vis-à-vis the state in the narrower sense merely means an expansion of the actors included in the analysis, but not a fundamental expansion of the privileges under consideration. This also leaves identity categories as interest groups invisible.

This does not apply only to Gramsci, but also to the decades of hegemony theorists who have built on him. Assuming that hegemony results from the relations of production and, moreover, not taking into account the micro-processes in power relations, the concept of hegemony, as in traditional Marxism, leads to a truncated and thus one-sided analysis of power. It leads to what Erik Borg (2001) calls the "double step": on the one hand, the economy is assumed to be determinant, especially when it comes to the emergence of the crisis, but then, in contrast, the way out of the crisis is presented as a solution strategy and thus as the result of intentional action by the elite. Thus, hegemony is reduced to the transmission mechanism of a stable development model. Christoph Scherrer (1997) criticises in particular the neo-Gramscian International Political Economy as tending to stylise hegemony as the sole result of top-down-imposed transnational elite discourses. The smaller the group with the power to act, the more this approach contains a structural anti-Semitic bias through its appeal to a secret world domination.

This double step also makes counter-hegemonic struggles invisible or at least presents them as ineffective or at best achieving very superficial changes. Mind you, this is all the more true in approaches where, unlike in the theory of hegemony, the claim to include all power relations is not formulated at all. At the same time, racism, sexism etc. are taken quite seriously nowadays, and in Marxist contexts are commonly formulated as not being side contradictions. In the late twentieth century, individual paragraphs on sexism and racism became the rule in many books critical of capitalism, and later entire chapters. But as long as all dynamics are explained by the capitalist mode of production, racist or sexist motivated struggles for hegemony do not exist according to the analysis. The category of gender thus remains external to the theory or is at best added mechanically, as Birgit Sauer puts it (2001:87).

In the spectrum of hegemony-theoretical regulation theory, it was Anja Ruf who first integrated the development of women's work into the (post-)Fordist analysis in her 1990 book *Frauenarbeit und Fordismus* [Women's Work and Fordism]: The first suburban settlements with so-called non-working housewives emerged in the 1920s because of the Fordist shift, which meant better-earning male workers. Often this did not even mean that women had not taken on paid employment, but always under the hegemonic myth of the "additional earner". Accordingly, Ruf sees as a strategic basis of Fordism the low-paid employment for women on the one hand, and their unpaid family work on the other. From historical research on trade union politics in the 20th century, it becomes clear that these relations were not seriously challenged by the male-led and shaped trade unions (Habermann 1997; 2019).

Since then, numerous feminist state theorists have written about the state as a male-dominated gender regime (e.g. Brigitte Young 1991) and more generally as "inevitably racialised as well as gendered and bourgeois" (Wendy Brown 1992:178). Especially European feminist scholars, particulary in the German speaking context and from the British school of International Political Economy (Gülay Çağlar 2022), have been using Nicos Poulantzas' Gramscian-inspired theory of the state (1978), which conceives of the state as the "material condensation of a relationship of forces", although for him it is still reduced to the relationship "among classes and class fractions" (Poulantzas 1978:129). Feminist state theorists extend this to gender and other power relations. Condensed in the state, these go beyond a direct depiction of the respective acute power relations and express themselves in the institutions of the state in the narrower sense. On the other hand, the state is conceived as relatively independent of acute power relations, and can thus also mean protection for victims of discrimination. But the essential moment is a strategic selectivity, according to which the state is not equally accessible to all societal forces and their goals, but this accessibility is inscribed in the state. Bob Jessop (2001) expands on this as a "strategic relational approach" and explicitly refers to "gender selectivities of the state".

In 1990, Ruf did not overlook the colonial and racist background of Fordism. Of course, the groundbreaking statement by the Black lesbian feminist socialist Combahee River Collective, published in 1977, introducing the term "interlinking" for what later would be known under the term intersectionality, but rooted in their critic of capitalist society, can be seen in this light, too. Also the fundamental work by Cedric Robinson on *Black Marxism* (1983) laid the foundation for many essential writings on racial capitalism.

Fordism represented an unfolded stage of white patriarchy, as it made white men in Europe and the USA the high-income and thus powerful strata of the wage-earning classes, while (white) women/people of colour were exposed to exploitation – albeit in a very unequal way. Cheap labour in the colonies or cheap labour of migrants as well as un- or underpaid women's work – and not so much male, white wage labour – were the essential foundations of capitalist development since the end of the 19th century. Only a linkage of exploitation according to racist, sexist and classist lines had made Fordist development possible.

In the image of the square representing the historical bloc of Fordism, women/people of colour would be either at the bottom or outside. The

Fordist welfare-state based on a class compromise allowed for white and male privilege. It was only in the rise of their movements in the 1960s that their interests found a significant voice in civil society discourse as a struggle for participation within the given system. This is then already concomitant with transition to neoliberalism.

Outside the hegemonic bloc

With regard to the colonies or the colonised subjects in the colonies, it can be argued that their position is to be placed outside the square. Gramsci writes about the "subaltern classes" in the peasant south of Italy in contrast to the developed proletariat in the north of Italy. To this day, the term subaltern is used in some neo-Marxist literature as a synonym for the working class (Candeias 2021). Spivak, in an interview with Leon de Kock (1992), is very clear on this point: "The working class is oppressed. It's not *subaltern*". She uses the expression in parallel to Gramsci's remarks to refer to those who are even further in the shadow, who do not even participate in hegemony in any way.

Against this binary thinking of "If I am oppressed, then I cannot belong to oppressors", Spivak is even more explicit in her attitude: "Many people want to claim subalternity. They are the least interesting and the most dangerous" (ibid.). This is what Stephan Lessenich considers the lifelong lie of the affluent left in capitalist society, and, with Rob Nixon, the power not to have to account for the consequences of one's actions. Indeed, not even having to take note of them.

The articulation of counter-hegemonic knowledge and thus transformation, accordingly, is made impossible by the subaltern positioning. *Can the Subaltern Speak?* is Spivak's famous essay (1988) and question. Spivak implicitly denies this. The subalterns cannot speak because they are outside the economic, political and cultural hegemony. Their counter-hegemonic knowledge lies outside the common sense, and therefore cannot be heard.

I will dare to list the reasons. Firstly, subalterns cannot speak, or rather here they are not heard, since their consent plays no role in the stability of the hegemonic relations; since they have "no strong arm", they also do not receive any material concessions. Secondly, they cannot articulate themselves in a counter-hegemonic way because they too are imbued with the hegemonic discourse. This means that often they themselves are not in a position to question normality. Thirdly, if they sufficiently overcome the hegemonic common sense in themselves through joint political analysis and action, what they would have to say to free themselves from their subaltern position (or rather to untie it and with it the societal structure that brings it about) lies outside the hegemonic reality and is not compatible with it. Because what they would have to say contains a dimension beyond the existing and societal thought. It would challenge the historical bloc as a whole. Today, and since the beginning of the market being a world system, this is true for the starving people, because they die from the hegemonic common sense not to question the market.

In the image of the square, those outside are subaltern. Although even from a European perspective, the times of the Fordist welfare-state class compromise in its pure form is over, the post-Fordist neoliberal, perhaps even post-neoliberal bloc still resembles the Fordist one in its basic features. As before, its wealth is still based on externalisation: formerly largely of the colonies, and later on what used to be called the "Third World" that nowadays is referred to as the Global South. But even if we were to stand on the threshold of an even greater geographical upheaval with a change in which nations are in which positions, this does not alter the fundamental representation as inside and outside of the hegemonic square within the historical bloc and its externalisations.

By taking into account the outside of the square, it becomes apparent that its inside can also be understood as a triangle: as the tip of the iceberg model. This triangle of the visible, monetary, civil societal sphere is only the tip of the bigger triangle: the whole of the economy. Here, down in the water, are the subaltern – and the whole oikeios, *to use Moore's term for the web of life, or, more concretely, for the naming of the web of relations by way of which humans (and other species) create the conditions of life.*

It is Stuart Hall who, within the hegemony theory framework, provides the micropolitical analyses of hegemonic struggles including racist and, following, sexist power relations.

Sex, race, class etc. are articulated

Born in Jamaica in 1932, Hall came to Oxford on a scholarship in 1951 and, as editor of the *Universities and Left Review,* took on a central role in the beginnings of the new, predominantly white left. He criticises the reduction to class as the sole contradiction as well as its neglect (Hall 1992a:400). As one of the founders of cultural studies in the UK, he investigates power relations with the aim of making their influence on cultural practices visible. Hall breaks down the dichotomy between a structuralist and a culturalist approach by showing culture as material practices.

Hall emphasises that Gramsci's understanding of hegemony as a consensus supported by all takes shape in the form of everyday action: People reproduce the relations recognised as "normal" through their daily routine. Hegemony is therefore always coupled with practices. Culture – understood as the field of practices, representations, languages and customs in every historical society – therefore represents for him one of the essential arenas where the struggle for leadership is fought out (Hall 1983).

Moreover, in his cultural studies, Hall works out both the mutability and the continuity of hegemonies. He emphasises that hegemony does not change in stages, i.e. in phases that can be clearly distinguished from one another. The processes of deconstruction and reconstruction, of linking and separating ideas, of articulation and disarticulation are complex. Since hegemony is constructed through complex processes of struggle and is never established once and for all, it must be constantly renewed and restaged (Hall 1988). At the same time, the attainment of hegemony never has only one face, but only one predominant tendency. Instead of assuming a succession of "historical blocs", only interrupted by organic crises, Stuart Hall emphasises that hegemony is always shifting (Hall 1992b:468).

Conversely, the recording of everyday actions also makes visible the continuities produced in everyday life. In Hall's research, for example, the paths perpetuating racism become clear: through the unquestioned or barely questioned small actions in everyday racist life. From Hall showing how much ideologies have been internalised and solidified as cultural practices, the permanent shifting becomes obvious in all its tenacity: repeated dayly, but as historically solidified forms.

The square (which is also a triangle) of the historical bloc called Fordism does not simply contain the same racism across the decades. More precisely, racism and other power relations are never the same on any given day – they are always shifting. In this way only, the results of struggles can also become visible. Nor has the post-Fordist, neoliberal bloc automatically produced a completely different racism. Despite economic upheavals, relations of power remain relatively stable in their everyday reproduction – and yet change every day. The historical blocs are no longer chronologically ordered next to each other, but one is morphing into the next.

This is where something comes together that is often controversial to this day: everyday racism, including language, is considered by many to be less important than struggles over material things. But it is not least in those areas traditionally excluded from "the political" that forms of domination are repeated and consolidated on a daily basis. Summing up this idea Gayatri C. Spivak writes: "The complicity between cultural and economic value systems is acted out in almost every decision we make" (Spivak 1987:166).

Hall's empirical approach, as well as his emphasis on both capitalism and racism, allows him to work out concretely how different and sometimes contradictory interests develop into historical blocs that remain fragile due to their internal contradictions. Since not only classes represent the actors, but also groups resulting from every societal division, new articulations can be captured analytically; such as the "white patriarchy" in Fordism as a class compromise on the basis of sexist and racist oppression and exploitation. Hall does not understand racism and sexism as relations of domination subordinate to capitalism, but explicitly examines them as forces driving action.

The exclusive linking of the concept of hegemony to the economy is inconsistent – this is key for Ernesto Laclau/Chantal Mouffe (1995) as well. They consider preventing the concentration of power at one point (for example, in a dictatorship of the proletariat) as the precondition for any truly democratic transformation of society. Accordingly, they believe to have only consistently unfolded the concept of hegemony, for which they further develop Gramsci's theory of hegemony with the help of post-structuralism based on Jacques Derrida's concept of deconstructivism. Hence, they transfer the basic post-structuralist idea that there is ultimately nothing essentialist to Gramsci's concept of hegemony, and introduce the term "Post-Marxism" as a theoretical approach.

Nevertheless, they understand their model as a materialist theory. They reject an interpretation of Marx that invokes the inner logic of a self-contained model in the name of materialism, because this would mean remaining attached to idealism and reducing reality to a model. On the contrary, they argue, the relational moment of materialist theory cannot be limited by an essentialist moment. For Laclau/Mouffe, a truly materialist theory consists "in a deepening of the relational moment" in Marx's thinking (Laclau/Mouffe 1990:112).

Laclau/Mouffe not only oppose the idea that economic developments have a determining effect on political ones. A distinction must be made between the relative weight of the economic space in the determination of social processes, and the nature and constitution of the economic space itself; this too is seen as an essentialism. All previous attempts to overcome economism were an editing of the scale, the essentialisation of the economy itself remained untouched. They see a second elementary core of essentialist fixations, which has banished the political imagination of the left, in the belief in a state takeover as a panacea. This etatism implies that there is a point of concentration of power from which society can be "rationally" reorganised. This view contradicts a radical democracy.

Apart from these essentialisms of economism and etatism, Laclau/Mouffe see as a third obstacle to radical democracy in Marxism what they call "classism": an understanding of the working class as a coherent actor. While etatism and economism initially seemed to have been overcome in Gramsci's work, through his understanding of hegemony and articulation, such classism can still be found in his work. This, however, would all of a sudden reintroduce statism and economism: For Gramsci, in the end, there could only ever be one unifying principle in any hegemonic formation, and this could only be one class, i.e. either the capitalist or the working class. But this reduces hegemonic struggles to class struggles on the one hand, and to a zero-sum game on the other. If one class does not win, the other wins. This they call the hidden essentialist core of Gramsci's thinking. For to claim that hegemony must always correspond to a fundamental economic class means, on the one hand, to reaffirm the determination by economics (economism) in the last instance, and, on the other hand, again to restrict power relations to the state (etatism) (Laclau/Mouffe 1985).

By understanding politics, like Gramsci, as articulation, i.e. in the connection of different power relations to the hegemonic position of a historical bloc, and by extending poststructural thinking, Laclau/Mouffe understand articulation as establishing links between elements, modifying their identity as a result. This means that in the process of articulation interests and identities undergo shifts or are produced (Laclau/Mouffe 1985:123ff).

They see this as an ambiguity already inherent in Gramsci's concept of the "war of position". Understanding relations with other societal forces as military implies always retaining one's own separate identity. At the same time, however, for Gramsci war of position meant the progressive disintegration of a civilisation and the construction of another. Thus, far from being fixed from the beginning, the identity of the opponents is constantly changing in the process.

The impossibility of structures to fully constitute themselves requires contingent decisions by the subject, which comes into being at the moment of decision. Such a transformation of one's identity and its context through contingent decisions is not a self-determined act. But there is room for articulation, through which in turn the discourses and the structures are altered. From this interplay of joint subversion of contingency and necessity a mutual determination of subjects and structure emerges. Conversely, the structures cannot close because the subject is incapable of repeating everything discursive (that is, all utterances and actions, all concealments and omissions) identically. Subject and structure no longer face each other separately, but in relation to each other, and are thus co-original (Laclau 1990:21).

Since every identity is contingently related to its conditions of existence, any change in one must entail a change in the other. As an example, Laclau cites a trade union as a collective subject whose relationship with the political system is drastically changed by a series of political and economic decisions; in this case, not the same trade union would exist in a changed context, but also a changed trade union (Laclau 1990:30). The same is true of the subjects in relation to each other, since they too are constantly undermined by their outside. Actors transform their own identity by seizing certain structural opportunities and not others. And here, too, any change in one identity entails changes in others.

Laclau/Mouffe include that these processes are not being carried out by identical subjects, but that identities change together with their contexts. Identities in a racist society will not be the same as in a society without racism. Oppressed people resisting will not be the same before and after resisting – and neither will their oppressors. The subject thus stands in a contingent relationship to its materialistic conditions insofar as the one would not be the same without the other (Laclau 2000:49). Interests as well as identities form or change in articulation.

And yet, Laclau/Mouffe ultimately fail to do justice to the complexity of power relations. In their 1985 book, again only power relations related to the process of accumulation are mentioned, and thus ultimately all others are disregarded. Precisely because of their realisation that in every articulation – and every action constitutes an articulation – identity is modified as a result, the extensive omission of identity categories is not understandable. Even if an individual is intent on their individual advantage, they will do so in a way that incorporates certain identities into their project – be it as a class, as a gender, as a "people", as a "race", as an "Aryan", etc. It is always group identities and thus identity categories that form the basis for participation in power; only in this way can a historical bloc emerge. However, Laclau even distances himself from theorists who tried to stick to the category "class" in their inclusion of identities in the analysis. And he does it in not very polite words (Laclau 2000a:296).

Be it class, gender or race etc., none of these identities can be thought without reference to the others. Only if there are capitalists, are there workers; only if there are men, are there women; only if there are whites, are there blacks, and the historically specific form of, for example, a female/white/citizen identity can only be thought of in relation to all other identity categories.

It is Judith Butler who unites the departure from the autonomous subject on a radically anti-essentialist basis with an explicit inclusion of embodied identity.

Hegemony constructs identity

The US philosopher Judith Butler also operates with the Gramscian concept of hegemony (albeit far less systematically than Laclau/Mouffe), and sees their own theory of performativity as not far removed from it: Both emphasised the way in which the social world is made and in which new societal possibilities emerge (Butler 2000:13f.). Butler's work *Gender Trouble* (1990) triggered not only a theoretical caesura, but also decisively third-wave feminism. Similar to Laclau/Mouffe's attempt to liberate Marxism from final essentialisms, it is concerned with transcending in feminism the notion of a natural sexed body that precedes discourse and thus an essential basis of sexism. It is about deconstructing what appears to be ontological or natural by showing the possibility of shifting this seemingly natural through alternative practices.

The distinction between (biological) sex and (social) gender was of great strategic importance in feminist theory in relation to prevailing biological determinisms: With the separation between sex and gender, it was pointed out that there was no causal connection between the two. However, Judith Butler problematises the sex/gender concept with its assumption of an unchanging, natural core of gender identity and its underlying binary frame of nature versus culture: It still presupposes a natural bodily substrate that is subsequently overformed. But gender cannot be "pure" in the sense of pre-social, because there can be no boundary where the "natural", sexual body begins, untouched by discourses. Within discourses, designations take place that are produced again and again in constant repetitions along discursive rules. This mechanism obscures the fact that the "natural" body does not lie before the signifying discourse, but is first brought forth through repeated representational acts in its respective designation, and is co-original with nature. The separation of sex and gender is the result of the modern split between nature and culture.

Butler warns against a personification of discourse in the sense of "the discourse constructs the subject": This merely means a simple inversion of the terms (Butler 1993a). (De)construction must mean more, precisely because "nature" is not the white sheet of paper that is shaped by discourse. The body is thus not an independent materiality shaped by power relations external to it, but it cannot be thought of without them. In this context, it also becomes clear why Butler explicitly places herself in the tradition of Michel Foucault, despite her concept of discourse, which is obviously influenced by Derrida: to emphasise the effect on corporeality and being, life as subject.

Foucault also pays particular attention to the institutional effects of discourse and their role in the constitution and domination of subjects. Foucault's concept of archaeology represents "intellectual excavation" (Norbert Finzsch) to buried discursive formations – or in other words: to the common sense of past epochs. In order to be able to analyse the transition from one to the other, Foucault develops the concept of genealogy. In doing so, he places power relations at the centre of his attention, defining them not as something external to economical or sexual etc. processes, but as deeply intervowen (Foucault 1976). He coins the term "governmentality" to pursue the processes of subjectivation in the connection between technologies of domination and technologies of the self (Foucault 1978, 1979). Thus, he assumes that pastoral governing techniques (understood as the "governing of souls") produce forms of subjectivation on which the modern state and capitalist society are built.

Judith Butler assumes with Foucault that juridical regimes of power also first produce the subjects ultimately represented by them (Butler 1990). Butler connects the impact of discourses with everyday performativity through which structures are reproduced, but also shifted. As with Derrida, in Butler's understanding a subject is constituted through a process of exclusion, in which regulating norms materialise through their enforced constant repetition. Over time, the repetitions constitute the hegemonic articulation as the only possible form without an alternative; the traces of this violent oppression are increasingly concealed. And yet this process can never be fully completed, because the bodies never fully conform to these norms. Also, no iteration can ever be identical. The other is always present in the form of cracks, and any identification is thus unstable. Butler emphasises that identification is often undermined by the unconscious. Unconsciously, ideals can be internalised to which the consciousness mind detests and fights against. For if the subject is brought forth through an exclusion, then it comes into being through a condition from which it is separated and distinguished by definition; desire, however, aims at the dissolution of the subject. These unintended consequences, not fully controllable by intention, would have unsettling and transformative effects (Butler 1997).

Like Laclau/Mouffe, Butler shows that power struggles do not emanate from identity categories but constitute them, and furthermore that shifts are not only possible but inevitable. At the same time, however, Butler emphasises subjects being inextricably linked with their embodied identities. By elaborating the tenacious adherence to a given identity, how rooted people are in what is also their embodied mode of existence, Butler also shows how difficult it is to shift structures (Butler 1998).

What can such a systematic inclusion of Butler's insights mean in the already gained intersectional and non-essentialist understanding of hegemony? It shows how hegemony (re-)constructs identity.[16] This is again visualised in the square.[17]

Our square (which is also the top of a triangle) now finally goes beyond the possibility of representation as a static model. Not only the individual historical blocs are shifting into the following historical bloc, not only are the subject positions shifting inside and outside the square (or between the upper and the lower part of the triangle), but the identities are also constantly changing. Not even a gif could display this: there is no going back, everything is constantly changing. But the video that has now become necessary for the representation needs a high resolution, because as long as subjects are in rigid structures, every shift remains laborious and hardly noticible.

Queering the material context

In view of the analysis suggesting that the subject cannot be detached from the societal and thus material context, and demonstrating that power relations or hegemonies cannot be thought of independently of identity categories, it is surprising how little Butler is dealing with this context, especially with economics. However, in the volume *Contingency, Hegemony, Universality. Contemporary Dialogues on the Left,* co-authored with Ernesto Laclau and Slavoj Žižek, Butler expresses their agreement

> that hegemony emphasizes the ways in which power operates to shape our everyday understanding of social relations, and to orchestrate the ways in which we consent to (and reproduce) those tacit and covert relations of power. Power is not stable or static, but is remade at various junctures within everyday life; it constitutes our tenuous sense of common sense, and is ensconced as the prevailing epistemes of a culture. Moreover, social transformation occurs not merely by rallying mass numbers in favour of a cause, but precisely through the ways in which daily social relations are rearticulated, and new conceptual horizons opened up by anomalous or subversive practices.
>
> *(Butler 2000:13f)*

Butler states elsewhere that while the embodied and domesticating possibilities of capital are immense, any theory that cannot think the possibilities of transformation from within the systemic formation is itself complicit with the idea of the eternal character of capital that it so readily produces (1998:255). For Butler, everyday relations must be re-articulated, that is, subversively undermined, in order to be able to open up new horizons. She describes it as a "paradoxical activity" to resist the very categories by which one is constituted (Butler 1993b). In this way, however, Butler largely equates agency with the subversion of identity. Adamczak's criticism in this regard has already been mentioned, that this harbours the danger of ontologising the societal context into a bad one and threatens to assume the unrevolutability of the conditions. Especially since in the old structures it is only possible to escape the invocations to a very limited extent, as Adamczak vividly illustrates: "Under prevailing conditions it usually seems more sensible not to strike but to work, not to denounce patriarchy but to fight one's own loneliness, not to steal but to go shopping, not to visit the plenum but to visit one's relatives" (2017:379; translation F.H.). Also those who like their relatives will understand.

Back again to the visualisation of the square – it now becomes a trash compactor: to the image by Gopal Dayaneni, explained in the introduction, in that a trash compactor symbolises our present situation in the face of climate change and other crises. The walls of the compactor, representing the crises, are coming closer and closer. More precisely: the square as a hegemonic bloc within the historical bloc becomes a square within a square, just as the triangle is also the tip of the iceberg and thus of a larger triangle. For in Dayaneni's comparison (unlike in the film), the trash compactor also includes the subalterns, the marginalised here in the literal sense: those who are the first to be crushed, since they are at the edges, while the privileged placements are at the centre. The marginalised try to penetrate into the interior, and those already located in the interior try to get even more into the centre. But this is not simply a fight of everyone against everyone. Those on the inside are already largely in agreement: Those from the margins, the others, should stay where they are.

But the moving force behind the walls is the market, or more precisely, the law of value. Everybody is threatened by being crushed by it, but how then does the trash compactor get moving? Chapter 3 shows historically how the construction of the market and thus the law of value came about. The energy behind the crises comes from everyday reproduction, iteration.

The fact that this is not so easily changeable is also represented by the term *Imperial Mode of Living* used by Ulrich Brand and Markus Wissen. With "mode of living" instead of "mode of life" they want to emphasise the structural element, without neglecting our individual limit of agency. However, a change in individual action alone does not lead to the abolition of these conditions. The law of value exposes all subjects, including the hegemonic, to structural constraints and is far from enabling agency even for the privileged in a liberal, voluntarist sense. But without the functioning of the individual, the law of value could of course not work. Just as identity (categories) emerge through (hegemonic) articulation, economic value also emerges only in the hegemonic reproduction of everyday doing capitalism.

Queering identity is not the only means of transformation. Certainly, the conditions change when I de-identify my gender or my invocation as an economic subject. Or is Butler aiming at the fact that when I put my "body on the line" (Butler 2000a:178), I will no longer be the same afterwards? It is precisely experiences of resistance that have a high self-transforming, queering effect on identities, whether through experiences of repression or through experienced solidarity. And undeniably, subject and structure are connected. Besides, there are undoubtedly important reasons to focus on one's own identity. But there is no transformational reason to start here. To reject the identity as a meat-eating person and become vegan is one approach; another is to fight with others to make vegan food a matter of course in one's own canteen or in society as a whole. Those who are vegan in their own canteen, although there are always only meat dishes, will perhaps only be pitied by everyone as a freak and might even give up again themselves. If the space can be altered, then it becomes easier for others to eat and become vegan, that is to say it becomes easier for the other subjects to articulate differently and to transform themselves by doing so.

Here the significance of "spaces of other logics" becomes clear (with Foucault 1984, these could be called "heterotopias"). If, to take another example, people can only think of two genders in their common sense, they will assign all deviations from this either to one or the other or perceive them as deviant. In subcultural queer spaces, the strange eyeing of whether a person also visually and habitually corresponds to what they aspire to be is gone. New articulations emerge that can also only be realised in spaces like these, and that in turn further transform these spaces. Compared to decades ago, a lot has happened in public awareness concerning queer identities (and the simultaneous rise in queer hostility is also a sign of this). To a large extent this was made possible by such "spaces of other logics". For a shifted (gender) identity is not made real in the morning in front of the wardrobe, but through the affirmative response of the subjects forming the space of self-evidence, i.e. fellow human beings. This is also why transformations cannot happen individually, but only collectively.

In this sense, subcultural "spaces of other logics", in which other practices can become reality and habitual alongside the claim of freedom from domination, are essential. This is no less true for spaces of other economic practices. The Bielefeld women, who are also called the subsistence theorists, argued in this sense for strengthening and expanding the field of subsistence. This has been sharpened as "dissident subsistence" (Schwertfisch 1997).

Nevertheless, these incomplete spaces are not the only fields of struggle for a different rationality. Crucial for societal transformation is the shifting of the common sense in terms of the war of position as a struggle for hegemony in civil society. However, this does not just mean a struggle for discourse in media of all kinds or in the use of language. As Laclau/Mouffe write, for Gramsci, war of position means the progressive disintegration of a civilisation and thus the construction of another civilisation. Thus, far from being fixed from the beginning, the identity of the opponents is constantly changing in the process. Even in the case of militant forms of resistance, it is essential to ask how much a change in common sense can be achieved with them. If a militant form of action brings about an affirmation of the existing, it will not be as effective as transformations taking place in everyday interpersonal relations, which then, for example, make it seem absurd to people to have to live in a competitive society with structural hatred (see chapter 4). Whatever form resistance may take, the aim is to alter the hegemonic common sense as far as possible, since any hegemony needs consensus. And for this, these new logics mostly will stem from heterotopias.

Such spaces of other logics emerge not least through articulations of the queer desires of subjects. In the beginning is the scream, as John Holloway puts it in his book *Change the World without Taking Power* (2002). In the beginning, there might be a "queer desire" to provide for oneself beyond the official economy, as described by Evangeline Heiliger, due both to precariousness and the pleasure those activities provide "for creating possibility and access using imagination, time, and repurposed goods" (2015:196). Forms as community gardening or community supported agriculture, circles of caring and sharing, where people contribute without exchange logic are collective examples of these desires. In places of resistance, be it in the occupied places of the Occupy movement, the Arabellion movement, or the forests occupied for protection from logging in Germany and the Zone to Defend in France, or struggles by indigenous peoples against the destructions of their land by extractivism, be it in Canada, Colombia or Nigeria: they all re/produce other logics of re/production.

But at the beginning, isn't it also the decision of individuals to get off the sofa? Does it make sense, by analogy with Spivak's "strategic essentialism", to invoke a "strategic voluntarism"? As analytically correct as it is that we are limited by structures, it is also clear that believing in the changeability of conditions contributes more to transformation than stopping at emphasising structures. We must not leave the field to supporters of neoliberalism with their appeal to subjects as effective agents – and thereby reproduce capitalism. Only pointing to the structures or to "those up there" as the powerful prevents activating one's transformative potential of doing.

Many feel uneasy about the cited representations of what we as subjects are. However, the core idea is also found in Karl Marx as the self-creation (autopoiesis) of the human being through societally changing activity. This has many names: activity, practices, doing, performativity or articulation – in any case, the historicity of being opens up possibilities for radical transformation.

Caring within the web of life

What the theories presented here have in common is accusing methodological individualism of assuming atomised subjects that negate any interdependence. It is all the more astonishing that – through the back door – such a concept reappears in Laclau's work. While Butler points with Spivak to the difficulty of having different recognitions as subjects through subaltern positions, Laclau does not share the concern regarding subjects and their unequal subject positions, on the contrary believing that they could articulate themselves with equal force. While Butler draws from Spivak's analysis a commitment to the other, Laclau rejects such a commitment and refers to the subject as "God" to indicate its sovereignty in decision-making (see Butler 2000a; Laclau 1996).

Derrida also assumes that in the encounter with the other, a person changes. For him, this gives rise to a new undecidability that forces further decisions. Such a real decision (yet at the same time a passive decision, since it is not actively made by a sovereign subject) only exists if the other breaks into the self, otherwise it would be reeling off a programmed, identical act.

This breaking into the other is reminiscent of Hartmut Rosa's concept of *resonance* (2016). With this concept, which is basically opposed to capitalist alienation, Rosa grasps the aliveness that arises through the response of the other – and this other can also be the wood from which I want to build a chair, and the wood does not simply want what I want, but from the relationship between wood and me a chair arises that turns out differently from what was expected in the business plan. This normally means loss of profit, and loss of profit means the threat of job loss or loss of competitiveness.

The capitalist logic of value strives for every resource to be exchangeable without any will of its own, and every resonance – even towards the work colleague who is busy with other thoughts today – stands in the way of the logic of utilisation. Capitalism turns resonance, turns the response of the other into a flaw in the system. This process is what Marx captured with alienation.

In his book *Change the World Without Taking Power*, John Holloway writes of a "*scream of refusal*", which "must also be a reaffirmation of doing, an emancipation of power-to" (2002:208). He bases this scream on Marxist grounds, and even Marx later no longer spoke of alienation, so as not to suggest that there was a natural subject beneath alienation. As in the post-structuralist account of what is externalised in the invocation to subjects, an invocation is not everything we are:

> The scream of insubordination is the scream of non-identity. 'You are', says capital to us all the time, classifying us, defining us, negating our subjectivity, excluding any future that is not a prolongation of the present indicative. 'We are not', we reply [...] 'we are not, we negate, we overflow the bounds of any concept'. It appears that we are, but we are not. That, at its most fundamental, is the driving force of hope, the force that corrodes and transforms that which is. We are the force of non-identity existing under the fetishised aspect of identity. Contradiction is non-identity under the aspect of identity.
>
> *(Holloway 2002:151)*

What it doesn't say here: The scream can also be triggered by racism or sexism etc. Racism, sexism, ableism etc. also say "You are" all the time, classifying us, defining us, negating our subjectivity. And subjects answer "we are not", "we overflow".

And the chicken, which is now on the plate as chicken nuggets, said the same. It was of no use to the chicken, because in this relationship the power relations are literally devastating. The justification here is also shifted to biological difference. Evidence that the DNA difference between us and chimpanzees or bonobos is smaller than that between them and the animal second closest to them (the gorilla),[1] or that crows pass a kind of marshmallow test (Hillemann et al. 2014) and ants the mirror test (Tricot/Cammaerts 2015) does not disturb the common sense, because it is usually assumed that there will be an explanation why anthropocentrism has not to be shaken. This is in common with any subaltern subject position.

Not limiting our understanding of the world to the human aspect is the challenge newly addressed by New Materialism. Let us remember:

After the death of nature (Carolyn Merchant 1980) as the web of life at the beginning of the modern era, NATURE emerged as an unvalued resource seemingly waiting to be appropriated – including the European female sex and all sexes in the colonies. Meanwhile, the struggle for emancipation, but also once again for privileges, has shifted the situation. Who or what is NATURE is a contingent result of this. But the principle remains: Exploitation is only possible through borders. Hegemony re/constructs identity – this also applies to the question of who is part of the kingdom of ends and who belongs to the kingdom of means.

If I had always wondered how it could be justified that my dog Rocco did not participate in the discourse, when I so obviously acted on his communication and articulation, Donna Haraway takes her dog as the starting point for the manifesto and the book *When Species Meet* (2003/2008). The fact that it is the same species is no coincidence, but due to the fact that – depending on the cultural context – dogs, like otherwise only cats, are currently found on both sides of this kingdom-frontier. This makes it easier in the common sense to communicate with them than with pigs, which have to eke out their lives almost exclusively in the kingdom of ends.

Haraway emphasises that organisms are not to be understood as isolated and discrete entities, but as "nature-cultural" complexes. Indeed, this can also be well illustrated by dogs. Despite frequently heard phrases like "dogs don't eat biscuits in nature", there are no dogs like Rocco (or others in our neighbourhoods) "in nature". Their whole being is an expression of nature-culture due to breeding, thwarted by contingency as well as the queering desire to mix other than according to the law of value.

And apropos of biology shaped according to the law of value: "The chickens we eat today are very different from those consumed a century ago. Today's birds are the result of intensive post-World War II efforts drawing on genetic material sourced freely from Asian jungles, which humans decided to recombine to produce the most profitable fowl. That bird can barely walk, reaches maturity in weeks, has an oversize breast, and is reared and slaughtered in geologically significant quantities (more than sixty billion birds a year). Think of this relationship as a sign of Cheap Nature" (Patel/Moore 2017:3f).

We fit the same pattern, when we think of the invocations to be an employable subject who takes care of their physical fitness. And here, too, other relations of domination can be the reason: The fact that my grandfather, who spent his twenties on Mafia Island, which belongs to

Tanzania, waited for years for my white grandmother to join him, even though they had only known each other for 14 days, may well testify to great love. But it would have been impossible to marry off to one of the thousands of black women living there at the time, so presumably – in its coming about via relations of domination – my biology follows the same pattern as Rocco's. This is precisely Butler's point. For Butler, too, subjects do not exist prior to their relationships. But why then the anthropocentric limitation or at least de-naming of the web of life? Has it crept into their theory to deny NATURE its historicity?

Like no other, Karen Barad stands for the material turn, which has challenged and enriched post-structuralism. The physicist calls the idea of inherent character traits of beings "represenationalism" (2003:804). Also continuing the groundwork laid by Foucault, Butler and Lévinas' ethics of responsibility, Barad not only advocates a consistently relational understanding of ontology, but also goes beyond the anthropocentric concept of the subject to encompass the full spectrum of possibilities of alterity. Barad coins the neologism "intraaction", in contrast to an understanding of interaction as a relationship between independently existing beings (2007; 2003:815).

While there are, as already cited, passages in Butler's work that ascribe an efficacy to nature, Barad nevertheless criticises their theory for assigning matter an ultimately passive role, arguing that Butler remains bound to the mind–matter dualism. Barad makes the case for understanding matter as active and as thoroughly historical. Not grounded in hegemony theory, but with reference to Butler, Barad asks "what matters and what is excluded from mattering" (2007:184). If there were a hegemony-theoretical component in Barad's work, this would make the web of life visible as included in the social processes shaped in a hegemonic way.

The subject is thus not simply constructed in relation to the other identity, nor only as part of the societal context, but in relation to the entire web of life. And the entire web of life is included in the discourse and is also shaped by it as well as shaping it. This is not in opposition to Butler, on the contrary. But the web of life, like the societal context, remains largely unnamed. In this respect, no other theory is needed through the inclusion of the web of life, only the overcoming of the – at least implicit – binary logic into the human and the more-than-human.

To say that animals cannot communicate and therefore we cannot know how they want to live equals saying if we are not able to understand someone's language gives us the right to eat them. As absurd as this comparison may seem to us today, such arguments parallel the debate in Spain in the 16th century about whether the indigenous peoples of the Americas were human beings. At the time, this was also discussed as a justification for their enslavement. "Ob die Weiber Menschen seyn" – whether women were humans was debated in the 17th century (Wunder 1991:25f). Just as women/people of colour were considered nature, it is the inability of the more-than-human subalterns to speak, imperceptible in the dominant discourse. And those who cannot respond – as Donna Haraway points out – are considered killable (2003/2008:78ff).

At the same time, she speaks of "Staying with the Trouble". It is the same idea that Derrida sums up with "Il faut bien manger", we must probably eat (Derrida 1998:419). In other words, there is no good life for all in the sense that thriving could include every being. But to the argument derived from this, which I hear more and more often, that if people didn't eat the pig, they would have to eat the spinach, I usually reply that according to this logic they might as well eat me. That may not be an adequate response, but maybe there isn't one. It is a challenge to ensure that the effort to overcome anthropocentric relations of domination does not lead to a return of the omnipotent white eye as a view from nowhere, as feared by Susanne Lettow (2014:104). Finding answers here cannot be done at a desk, but only in resonance with the entire spectrum of alterity.

Putting caring at the centre opens the view and at the same time makes action concrete. On the one hand, inclusion of caring opens up the entire web of life. And now it also becomes even more obvious why structures can never remain identical: There is always birth and death and becoming in intraaction. Even with the beings that are part of us, we are always in change. For this reason alone, no iteration can be pure, which is why there are always breaks and openings in the structure, even if they are always very different in size. On the other hand, action becomes concrete, because unlike the big words of transformation or even revolution, the focus on caring makes it clear that our next decision is relevant here and now. The day before writing this I heard an intensive care doctor (whose name I unfortunately did not ask) contributing to a discussion that her need to be able to care for her patients well turns her radical.

To care is not a one-way process. Beyond the terms care-giver and care-receiver, resonance also opens up the perspective in caring that every relating, every questioning attention, every articulation is a "becoming-with" (Haraway 2016:221). And again, "unlearning privileges" is essential.

Such must be part of, to use another of Haraway's neologisms, response-ability. Privileges will dissolve as long as caring is conceived as response-ability, as going into resonance, as "unlearning one's privileges as one's loss". That is to understand that, yes, you are privileged – "But something is missing", to use Bert Brecht's phrase.

This has consequences for activism, too: "If you have come here to help me you are wasting your time, but if you have come because your liberation is bound up with mine, then let us work together", is the famous formulation of Lilla Watson that was the opening quote from the Peoples' Global Action manifest. At that time, she herself pointed out that it was short-sighted to attribute this quote to her, as it was born out of the collective process of a group of Aboriginal activists.

The place of politics is everywhere, the time for change is now, and emancipation is always the emancipation of others. The square of the historical bloc and the triangle that is an iceberg get in motion. Is a circle forming? Do we recognise the earth called Pachamama emcompassing all of us? Nope, it's not a circle. It is the web of life, overflowing with queer desires, from rigidity into aliveness.

Stop! We are still in the trash compactor! Not only are we far from being able to care for each other, to care for and within the web of life, but the compactor walls are inexorably closing in on all of us. How we got into it is the subject of the following chapter.

Note

1 Cf. https://www.wissen.de/bildwb/menschenaffe-und-mensch-eng-verwandt (15.06.2023).

References

Adamczak, Bini (2017) *Beziehungsweise Revolution. 1917, 1968 und kommende*, Frankfurt/M.: Suhrkamp.

Barad, Karen (2003) "Posthumanist Performativity. Toward an Understanding of How Matter Comes to Matter", *Signs. Journal of Women in Culture & Society*, 28 (3), 801–831.

Barad, Karen (2007) *Meeting the Universe Halfway. Quantum Physics and the Entanglement of Matter and Meaning*, Durham/London: Duke University Press.

Borg, Erik (2001) *Projekt Globalisierung. Soziale Kräfte im Konflikt um Hegemonie*, Hannover: Offizin.

Brand, Ulrich/Wissen, Markus (2017) *The Imperial Mode of Living. Everyday Life and the Ecological Crisis of Capitalism*, London/New York: Verso, 2021.
Brown, Wendy (1992) "Finding the Man in the State", in: *States of Injury. Power and Freedom in Late Modernity*, Princeton: University Press, 166–196.
Butler, Judith (1990) *Gender Trouble. Feminism and the Subversion of Identity*, New York/London: Routledge.
Butler, Judith (1993a) *Bodies That Matter. On the Discursive Limits of Sex*, New York/London: Routledge.
Butler, Judith (1993b) "Ort der politischen Neuverhandlung. Der Feminismus braucht 'die Frauen', aber er muß nicht wissen, 'wer' sie sind", in: *Frankfurter Rundschau*, 27.07.1993.
Butler, Judith (1995) "For a Careful Reading", in: Seyla Benhabib/Judith Butler/Drucilla Cornell/Nancy Fraser, *Feminist Contentions. A Philosophical Exchange*, New York/London: Routledge, 127–143.
Butler, Judith (1997) *The Psychic Life of Power. Theorie in Subjection*, Stanford: Stanford University Press.
Butler, Judith (1998) "Weitere Reflexionen zu Hegemonie und Gender", in: Oliver Marchart (ed.), *Das Undarstellbare der Politik. Zur Hegemonietheorie Ernesto Laclaus*, Wien: Turia+Kant, 254–257.
Butler, Judith (2000) "*Restating the Universal: Hegemony and the Limits of Formalism*", in: Judith Butler/Ernesto Laclau/Slavoj Žižek, *Contingency, Hegemony, Universality. Contemporary Dialogues on the Left*, London/New York: Verso, 11–43.
Butler, Judith (2000a) "*Competing Universalities*", in: Judith Butler/Ernesto Laclau/Slavoj Žižek, *Contingency, Hegemony, Universality. Contemporary Dialogues on the Left*, London/New York: Verso, 136–181.
Candeias, Mario (ed.) (2021) *KlassenTheorie. Vom Making und Remaking*, Hamburg: Argument.
Çağlar, Gülay (2022) "Decentering Political Authority and Power. Feminist Global Governance Studies in Europe", in: Maria Stern/Ann E. Towns (eds), *Feminist IR in Europe. Knowledge Production in Academic Institutions*, Cham: Palgrave Macmillan.
Derrida, Jacques (1998) "'Man muss wohl essen' oder die Berechnung des Subjekts", in: Jacques Derrida, *Auslassungspunkte. Gespräche*, Wien: Passagen, 267–298.
Foucault, Michel (1976) *The Will to Knowledge*, London: Penguin Books.
Foucault, Michel (1978) *Sicherheit, Territorium, Bevölkerung. Geschichte der Gouvernementalität I*, Frankfurt/M.: Suhrkamp, 2004.
Foucault, Michel (1979) *Die Geburt der Biopolitik. Geschichte der Gouvernementalität II*, Frankfurt/M.: Suhrkamp2004.
Foucault, Michel (1984) "Of Other Spaces. Utopias and Heterotopias", *Architecture Movement Continuité*, 5, 46–49.
Gramsci, Antonio (1929–33) *Gefängnishefte. Kritische Gesamtausgabe*, edited by Klaus Bochmann/Wolfgang Fritz Haug, Hamburg/Berlin, 1971–. Selections in

English, *The Antonio Gramsci Reader: Selected Writings, 1916–1935*, edited by David Forgacs, New York: Schocken Books, 1988.

Habermann, Friederike (1997) "Ökonomische Diskriminierung im 20. Jahrhundert – Geschlecht und Arbeit in Deutschland zwischen Theorie und Empirie", unpublished study for Museum der Arbeit, Hamburg.

Habermann, Friederike (2019) "Gewerkschaft als transformative Kraft. Das Beispiel der kanadischen Postgewerkschaft CUPW", RLS-online Paper: www.rosalux.de/publikation/id/42351/gewerkschaft-als-transformative-kraft (15. 06. 2023).

Hall, Stuart (1983) "The Problem of Ideology – Marxism without Guarantees", in: David Morley/Kuan-Hsing Chen (eds), *Stuart Hall – Critical Dialogues in Cultural Studies*, London/New York: Routledge, 1996, 25–46.

Hall, Stuart (1988) "The Troat in the Garden. Thatcherism among the Theorists", in: Cary Nelson/Lawrence Grossberg (eds), *Marxism and the Interpretation of Culture*, London: Macmillan, 35–57.

Hall, Stuart (1992a) "Cultural Studies and the Politics of Internationalization: An Interview with Stuart Hall by Kuan-Hsing Chen", in: David Morley/Kuan-Hsing Chen (eds), *Stuart Hall – Critical Dialogues in Cultural Studies*, London/New York: Routledge, 1996, 392–408.

Hall, Stuart (1992b) "What is this 'Black' in Black Popular Culture?", in: David Morley/Kuan-Hsing Chen (eds), *Stuart Hall – Critical Dialogues in Cultural Studies*, London/New York: Routledge, 1996, 465–475.

Haraway, Donna (2003/2008) *When Species Meet*, Minneapolis: University of Minnesota Press.

Haraway, Donna (2016) *Staying with the Trouble. Making Kin in the Chthulucene*, Durham/London: Duke University Press.

Heiliger, Evangeline (2015) "Queer Economies. Possibilities of Queer Desires and Economic Bodies (because 'the economy' is not enough)", in: Nikita Dhawan/Antke Engels/Christoph H.E. Holzhey/Volker Woltersdorff (eds), *Global Justice and Desire. Queering Economy*, Florence/KY, USA: Taylor and Francis, 195–212.

Hillemann, Friederike/Thomas Bugnyar/Kurt Kotrschal/Claudia A. F. Wascher (2014) "Waiting for Better, not for More: Corvids Respond to Quality in Two Delay Maintenance Tasks", *Animal Behavior*, 90, 1–10.

Holloway, John (2002) *Change the World without Taking Power*, London: Pluto Press.

Jessop, Bob (2001) "The Gender Selectivities of the State", e-text available at Department of Sociology, Lancaster University: https://www.lancaster.ac.uk/fass/resources/sociology-online-papers/papers/jessop-gender-selectivities.pdf (15. 06. 2023).

Kock, Leon de (1992) "Interview With Gayatri Chakravorty Spivak: New Nation Writers Conference in South Africa", *ARIEL: A Review of International English Literature* 23 (3)29–47.

Laclau, Ernesto (1990) "New Reflections on the Revolution of Our Time", in: Ernesto Laclau (ed.), *New Reflections on the Revolution of Our Time*, London/New York: Verso, 3–85.

Laclau, Ernesto (1996) "Dekonstruktion, Pragmatismus, Hegemonie", in: Chantal Mouffe (ed.), *Dekonstruktion und Pragmatismus*, Wien: Passagen, 1999, 111–154.

Laclau, Ernesto (2000) "Identity and Hegemony. The Role of Universality in the Constitution of Political Logics", in: Judith Butler/Ernesto Laclau/Slavoj Žižek, *Contingency, Hegemony, Universality. Contemporary Dialogues on the Left*, London/New York: Verso, 44–89.

Laclau, Ernesto (2000a) "Constructing Universality", in: Judith Butler/Ernesto Laclau/Slavoj Žižek, *Contingency, Hegemony, Universality. Contemporary Dialogues on the Left*, London/New York: Verso, 281–307.

Laclau, Ernesto/Chantal Mouffe (1985) *Hegemony and Socialist Strategy. Towards a Radical Democratic Politics*; quoted from *Hegemonie und radikale Demokratie. Zur Dekonstruktion des Marxismus*, Vienna, 2000.

Laclau, Ernesto/Chantal Mouffe (1990) "Post-Marxism without Apologies", in: Ernesto Laclau (ed.), *New Reflections on the Revolution of Our Time*, London/New York: Verso, 97–132.

Lessenich, Stephan (2016) *Neben uns die Sintflut. Die Externalisierungsgesellschaft und ihr Preis*, Berlin: Carl Hanser Verlag. Translated as *Living Well at Other's Expense. The Hidden Costs of Western Prosperity*, Medford: Polity Press, 2019.

Lettow, Susanne (2014) "Sehnsucht nach Unmittelbarkeit. Zur Konjunktur des politischen Vitalismus", *Femina Politica* 23, 2, 97–106.

Merchant, Carolyn (1980) *The Death of Nature*, San Francisco: Harper.

Nixon, Rob (2011) *Slow Violence and the Environmentalism of the Poor*, Cambridge, MA: Harvard.

Patel, Raj/Moore, Jason W. (2017) *A History of the World in Seven Cheap Things. A Guide to Capitalism, Nature, and the Future of the Planet*, Oakland: University of California Press.

Poulantzas, Nicos (1978) *State, Power, Socialism*, London: New Left Books.

Rosa, Hartmut (2016) *Resonanz. Eine Soziologie der Weltbeziehung*, Frankfurt/M.: Suhrkamp.

Ruf, Anja (1990) *Frauenarbeit und Fordismus-Theorie*, Frankfurt/M.: n.p.

Sauer, Birgit (2001) *Die Asche des Souveräns. Staat und Demokratie in der Geschlechterdebatte*, Frankfurt/New York: Campus.

Scherrer, Christoph (1997) "Eine diskursanalytische Kritik der Regulationstheorie", *Prokla. Zeitschrift für kritische Sozialwissenschaft*, 100, 457–482.

Schwertfisch (1997) *Zeitgeist mit Gräten. Politische Perspektiven zwischen Ökologie und Autonomie*, Bremen: yetipress.

Spivak, Gayatri Chakravorty (1987) *In Other Worlds: Essays in Cultural Politics*, London/New York: Routledge.

Spivak, Gayatri Chakravorty (1988) "Can the Subaltern Speak?", in: Patrick Williams/Laura Chrisman (eds), *Colonial Discourse and Post-Colonial Theory. A Reader*, New York: Columbia University Press, 1994, 66–111.

Tricot, M./Cammaerts, Roger (2015) "Are Ants (Hymenoptera, Formicidae) Capable of Self Recognition?" *Journal of Science*, 5, 521–532.

Wunder, Heide (1991) "Überlegungen zum Wandel der Geschlechterbeziehungen im 15. und 16. Jahrhundert aus sozialgeschichtlicher Sicht", in: Heide Wunder/Christina Vanja (eds), *Wandel der Geschlechterbeziehungen zu Beginn der Neuzeit*, Frankfurt/M.: Suhrkamp.

Young, Brigitte (1991) "Der Staat – eine 'Männerdomäne'? Überlegungen zur feministischen Staatsanalyse", in: Elke Biester et al. (eds), *Staat aus feministischer Sicht*, Berlin: Selbstverlag, 1992, 7–18.

3

CONSTRUCTION OF THE MARKET ECONOMY AND ITS SUBJECTS

In her book *The Origin of Capitalism: The Longer View* (2002), Ellen Meiksin, Wood points out that, paradoxically, in most accounts of the origin of capitalism, there is no origin at all. Instead, it is assumed that it has always existed and that it only needed to be freed from its chains – feudalism, for example – to allow it to grow and mature. Exchange has more or less always existed, and it seems as if the capitalist market were simply more of the same. Wood formulates in an ironic way: "History's journey to that final destination, to 'commercial society" or capitalism, has, to be sure, been long and arduous, and many obstacles have stood in its way. But its progress has nonetheless been natural and inevitable" (2002:12). This idea, according to anthropologist David Graeber in his book *Debt* (2011) is important for the myth that "the economy" is simply the realm in which humans can indulge their natural inclination to trade and barter: Since we have always traded and exchanged, we will always do so in the future (as long as no coercive regime prevents us from doing so). Thus, something like "the economy" would seem to exist, seemingly functioning independently of moral and political life according to its own rules. And insofar as people's actions in this area are significant, they only seem "rational" as long as they are guided by these moral values – which are quite contrary to the other areas of human coexistence. Money, in this view, is simply the most effective means (Graeber 2011:27ff). Such ahistorical naturalisation, Wood again

DOI: 10.4324/9781003373360-3

argues, limits our understanding of the past, for it denies not only the specificity of capitalism, but also the long and painful process that produced it. In doing so it also limits our hopes and expectations for the future (2002:16).

In this sense, the construction of ownership, labour and exchange will be traced in the following, as well as the construction of the economic subject, economic man. Linked to this was the construction of its racialised, gendered others, whereby the women's movement and the civil rights and other anti-racist movements achieved that the image of economic man was also extended to them. Or to put it another way: they could become part of the civil society struggling for privileges and thus be located inside the hegemonic bloc. But this does not change the externalisation structure of the market economy. Therefore, as contingent results in the struggle for hegemony and equality as inclusion in civil society, new and old exclusions are connected: along class and nationality, and not least along the successful performance of being able to conform to the image of economic man.

Commons turn into ownership

The German legal language (not so everyday speech) distinguishes "Besitz" (translated as "possession" in the following) from "Eigentum" (translated as "ownership" in the following). To illustrate: A tenant is the possessor of a flat, the landlady the owner. This distinction is fundamental when it comes to understanding that our current view of property is a naturalised construction. It was only in the late 17th century that the concept of ownership was given legitimacy beyond relations of force or God-given order by John Locke. For "ownership", in contrast to "possession", contains two additional rights: firstly, the right to exclude others from using a thing, even if one does not need it oneself. Secondly, the right to destroy it.

Rosa Luxemburg (1925) was probably not so wrong when she wrote of village communism as a typical form of human society that had been discovered in many parts of the world. This is now well known for indigenous modes of reproduction. Luxemburg, however, was also referring to peasant ways of life in Europe as late as the Middle Ages. Nowadays, the traditional notion of feudalism as a societal form of the unfree has been challenged in historical research (see also Brown 1974; Reynolds 1994). Many terms we associate with the feudal Middle Ages originate in modern times and represent backward projections. For example, the German term “Leibeigener” (serf) is first documented for 1645 – well into modern times. Silvia Federici, although cautioning against idealising these conditions, also points out in *Caliban and the Witch* that in the European countryside, decisions were made in self-governance (2004:43f). In village assemblies, decisions were made on the use of forest, water and pastureland as well as on the cultivation of arable land; in many cases, land possession rotated in the process.

Luxemburg was probably also right when she said that under Charlemagne, i.e. around the year 800, despite the size of his empire (encompassing a large part of today’s Western Europe), the economic laws were quite simple and could be understood by the dumbest peasant, for the ruthless demanding of the harvest products and, if necessary, the services were done directly (1925:53f). In addition to the narrative of a divinely ordained order, it was the direct power of the nobles, who at that time often roamed with army, bag and baggage, that forced these levies. Land ownership was not the reason – because the land was commons. In the medieval belief, everything belonged to God, even if he had left the goods to the people for “usufruct”.

What the peasants knew, they shouted out loud to the world in the Peasants’ Wars. But it was not only peasants who fought against injustice. “Eynem idern nach seyner notdorft ausgeteylt werden nach gelengenheyt” (It should be handed out to each according to their need after opportunity) – this is what the priest Thomas Müntzer fought for together with many other people in 1525.[1] Martin Luther’s reaction to this struggle is well known: Whoever could, should beat them to death like a mad dog, strangle and stab them, secretly and publicly.[2] That is exactly what was done. Alone 6,000 were slain in the course of a truce broken for this purpose on 15 May 1525 near Frankenhausen in Germany (Klein 1975:73). Müntzer himself was captured in the process and tortured in the presence of Duke George the Bearded; the confession comes from this situation. Two days later he was publicly beheaded, his body and head impaled separately. In all, tens of thousands were slaughtered. However, this so-called “Peasants’ War” was only the bloodiest climax, and perhaps also the endpoint, of countless rebellions during the transition to capitalism in Central Europe. In England, however, more than a hundred years later the movement of the true levellers or diggers followed in the course of the civil war.

For the implementation of the idea of ownership, the nobility fell back on the concept of *dominium*, which had arisen in the context of the Roman Empire. The term appears in Roman law towards the end of the Republic, around the time when hundreds of thousands of prisoners came to Italy as forced labourers and Rome consequently became a slave-holding society. The idea was derived from patriarchy, specifically from the male supremacy of the man as head of the household. This later went so far that a "pater familias" was allowed to execute slaves. Until then, property could not simply be destroyed, therefore this demanded a conceptual innovation in Roman law in order to legally grasp this de facto right. This logic was then extended to objects (Graeber 2011:211f).

However, it took another thousand years for this idea of unrestricted power of disposal to permeate northern Europe. With the concept of *dominium*, it became possible to demand rent from peasants without making it look like robbery. With the Magna Carta in 1215 and the Charter of the Forest in 1217 in England, the rights of the nobility as well as the rights of the commoners, i.e. the peasant population, not least to the use of the commons, began to be recorded in writing. These rights increasingly shifted in favour of the nobility (Million 2018). The transformation of compulsory labour into monetary payments, which began with the concept of ownership, had a liberating element for the better-off peasants, but the poorer ones, with less land, got into a debt spiral and in this way lost their livelihood. Representatives of the so-called "political Marxism", such as Wood, analyse this as the beginning of the market society. For this, societies with a market (like the peasants going to a market in the city to sell and buy a few products) are to be distinguished from a market society in which the market acts as an imperative and puts people in permanent competition with each other. As more land came under this economic order, those tenants who could produce competitively and pay good rents by increasing their own productivity (and expanding their market) increasingly had an advantage. The most competitive tenants gained access to even more land, while others lost the fields they cultivated altogether. This was because the lord of the manor's income depended on the economic success of the peasants; thus, the landlords had the incentive to spur their tenants, or force them as far as possible, to increase labour productivity (Wood 2002:118).

Later, the land was looted for use mainly as sheep pasture and fenced off by the nobility, combined with the demolition of villages, which drove people into the cities as the future proletariat. Wood argues that this rural transformation was considered by Marx to be the "original accumulation" not because it created a critical mass of wealth (as had often been the case in history), but firstly because the robbery of the commons forced the landless (free) peasantry to sell their labour power, and secondly because in the course of this new economic imperatives were generated, in particular the constraints of competition and the systematic need to develop the productive forces. This led to laws of motion the world had never seen before (Wood 2002:50).

Moore sees as decisive elements for the emergence of capitalism: 1) the extraction of a part of human activities as paid work; 2) the devaluation of the rest of nature, so that it can be put to work for free or at low cost; and 3) the regulation of the boundary that emerges between capitalisation and appropriation, between "economy", the relations that condition it and the web of life. With a view to the colonies, where this was also implemented and even more violently, he assumes a beginning of capitalism from 1450 (Moore 2015:98f).

Emphasising this upheaval of living conditions, Wood points out that this also means that the term "enclosure" should be understood not only in its literal meaning as the fencing in of common land or "open fields", but above all as the abolition of common and customary rights of use on which many people depended for their livelihood (2002:127). Silvia Federici defines "enclosure" even more broadly not only as the destruction of commons and the abolition of community rights, but thus also as the destruction of societal relations (2004:10).

Triggered by the removal of the possibility of subsistence, capitalism is characterised by the existence of an all-encompassing one-dimensional value system: the logic of exchange. The feudal economy and the supposedly divine order had had their day, but the appropriation of other people's labour had not. Hence Luxemburg's argument that more complicated economic laws were needed to make them more opaque. And the adoption of the dominium concept was not without a theoretical superstructure – even if this did not take place until the Enlightenment.

Those "not capable of any property" become the other

John Locke's *Two Treatises on Government* from 1689, or more specifically the second "An Essay Concerning the True Origin, Extent, and End of Civil Government", is considered a turning point in secular law.

Nature understood as a commons was also his starting point. The following paragraph is considered central:

> Though the Earth, and all inferior Creatures be common to all Men, yet every Man has a *Property* in his own *Person*. This no Body has any Right to but himself. The *Labour* of his Body, and the *Work* of his Hands, we may say, are properly his. Whatever then he removes out of the State that Nature has provided, and left it in, he has mixed his *Labour* with, and joyned to it something that is his own, and thereby makes it his *Property*. It being by him removed from the common state Nature placed it in, he hath by this *labour* something annexed to it, that excludes the common right of other Men. For this *Labour* being the unquestionable Property of the Labourer, no man but he can have a right to what that is once joyned to, at least where there is enough, and as good left in common for others.
>
> *(II § 27)*

Locke not only starts from the common sense that the earth be common to all men, but also considers it necessary to point out at the end that this right to exclusion is not an unconditional one, but must be put in relation to whether or not others have to suffer deficiency as a result. Basically, this still only legitimised possession rights, not ownership, and corresponded to commons rights. An understanding according to which a few individuals can own as much as the poorer half of the world's population – almost one billion of whom are threatened by malnutrition in their right to life and healthy development, and are responsible for every second case of infant mortality – should therefore also have been rejected by the pioneer of property.

But John Locke's argument takes another turn. For him, one's own property – Locke now switches from the third to the first person – also includes "the grass my horse has bit; the turfs my servant has cut" (II § 28). This shows, firstly, that in the end it is not the labour of the immediate producers that establishes ownership of the fruits of labour in bourgeois society. The myth that property is the reward for labour in capitalism is thus already exposed as such in its origin. Instead, for Locke there are people "not capable of any property" (II § 85). For this he names enslaved people and servants, but nothing else should apply to indigenous people and women. These "cannot in that state be considered as any part of civil society; the chief end whereof is the preservation of property" (II §

85). In other words, the state is there to protect property, and this property does not belong to all identity categories – not to all those who became the Other of the white male bourgeois.

Secondly, this reveals what in fact the innovation was. Locke was not the first to argue that unoccupied land could be claimed by those who could make it fertile – this had already been stated in the Charter of the Forest 1217 as the 12th Article. Locke's theory of property, however, introduced a hugely significant innovation. In his discussion of the value of a piece of land in the Americas, he was not interested in the amount of labour required for its maintenance by an indigenous person, but only in the fact that it yielded no profit, no exchange value. Ultimately, Locke's argument for the right to property was not the work expended by a person, but its use for the market. What really distinguishes his theory is the linking of labour and property to the creation of exchange value.

This implicit distinction also legitimised the conquest of commons-based and commons-creating cultures and economies, people and lands that fell victim to Western colonialism. Collective maintenance activities, even more so in the generally less visible, less destructive ways of indigenous cultivation, were not recognised as "labour". With this artifice, the English bourgeois revolutionaries bridged the gap between the claim to freedom and equality of all people, on the one hand, and their own colonial striving for power, on the other.

Anything done outside of labour becomes leisure

It was their sacred duty as a government to bring the people of Africa out of laziness and idleness, said Cecil Rhodes, mining monopolist and prime minister of south-eastern Africa, which had been declared a colony, at the end of the 19th century. The black people living there should finally realise the dignity of labour. Even at the beginning of the 20th century and after his death, the Rhodesian mining society let it be known that education, which corresponded to the status of Africans, should first and foremost inculcate the virtues of order, discipline and obedience, so that the indigenous would finally become useful to "his" employer and get used to seeing labour as the natural way of earning a living (Gronemeyer 1991a:11; Gronemeyer 1991b:18).

But of course, there was nothing natural about labour. The fact admitted in the quotation that the Blacks did not see labour as something natural already proves it; after all, they all had functioning economies. On the contrary: As in other parts of the world, also in Africa the phenomenon of permanent mass misery and mass hunger only arose in the aftermath of colonisation.

In the middle of the 19th century, Earl Grey (nowadays rather known for the tea variety) propagated the decisive two steps for getting Africans to work on the plantations. His effective double strategy was to first take away their land and secondly to raise taxes. Then they would be available as workers. In the somewhat later words of Lord Delamare, the first step must address the problem that as long as Africans had a sufficient piece of land to call their own and on which they could settle, the problem of a satisfactory supply of workers could not be solved. The best way to solve this is direct appropriation of the land, and in British East Africa Delamare led by example: in his case it was 150,000 acres. The second step was necessary to enforce a cash requirement. For this, again Cecil Rhodes also described the payment of a labour tax as the only way to get a grip on the people. And so, soon after the arrival of the pioneers in Rhodesia, colonial officials could be seen busily collecting a cottage tax. Since hardly anyone had cash, taking up wage labour was inevitable from that moment on (Gronemeyer 1991:10/42).

Labour as an abstraction came only late into the languages, including the European ones. Yet in all of these, labour has a basic meaning that emphasises the laborious and often also a relationship of dependence: Russian "*rabot*" is derived from "*rab*", the slave; the French *travail* and the Spanish *trabajo* from *tripalim* ("three-pole"), which was first a device for taming horses and as "tripulare" later a method of torture; and while "labour" in Anglo-Saxon is a paid activity, in Austria it is labouring from illness, for originally it stood for "staggering under a heavy load". Forced labour, workhouses, the expropriation of the land and its treasures, the destruction of social connections, the serialisation and instrumentalisation of the body, the implantation of a rigid consciousness of time, and education in order, punctuality and obedience – these were not only the ingredients of the colonial grand attempt to convert black people to the gospel of labour, these were also already the imperatives with which the labour society was once enforced in Europe (Gronemeyer 1991).

In other words, the workhouse disappeared because the whole of Europe became one. Idleness was first regarded as theft, later increasingly as incapacity, and labour became first a duty and then the purpose of life. The treadmill on which people had to work in the early modern era was internalised, into the mental inventory of the working person. And for the people of today who are caught in the treadmill it looks like a job ladder.

What always existed were words that denoted concrete activities. But not the abstraction detached from concrete references, which emphasises the laborious and the economic necessity and often arises from a relationship of dependence. It has nothing to do with inner motivation to do something or to see something done, only with the economic compulsion to do it. How this even destroys inner motivation will be discussed further under the consequences of the market economy in chapter 4.

Anything given outside of exchange logic becomes irrational or attributed to NATURE

Money has a lot to do with both ownership and labour. With ownership as distinct from possession which allows to exclude others from something without using it oneself, and then demand labour or money for it. With labour as opposed to activity: What is defined as labour requires external, "extrinsic" motivation, i.e. motivation that has nothing to do with the actual activity. And in the end this functions, because even when we do not feel it, somewhere there are those for whom money is blackmail.

The message "without money there can only be a primitive barter economy" has been hammered home so rigorously that we can no longer imagine anything else. It is inconvenient to exchange food for shoes when the cobbler needs a knife and the blacksmith would also rather have a jumper than vegetables, and so on and so forth: I learned this from a cartoon programme as early as preschool age, and it is still repeated today in introductions to economics. In his study on the origins of money *Debt*, the anthropologist David Graeber pokes fun at this, asking who in their right mind would open a grocery store under such circumstances? Graeber points out that for centuries researchers have been looking for this fabled land of barter – to no avail. Quite to the contrary, he says, it can be determined: Different cultures had very different economic forms. However, what did not occur was barter in the implied economic sense as equivalent exchange. Before the introduction of money (driven by the colonies), there is no society within which individuals would have exchanged goods in this way. Examples of barter can only be found in encounters between strangers who will most likely never see each other again and between whom there will certainly be no regular contact (Graeber 2011:38).

The main thesis of Graeber's book is that money did not arise from relations of exchange but from relations of debt – taxes being one them. And from this perspective, the crucial characteristic of money is its ability to transform morality into a matter of impersonal arithmetic, justifying things that would otherwise seem outrageous or obscene (Graeber 2011:20). According to Graeber, the one thing that history clearly shows is that there is no better way of defending and morally justifying relationships based on violence than to clothe them in the language of debt – especially because then the victim immediately appears to be in the wrong. Mafiosi knew this. So do the commanders of invading armies. For many thousands of years, violent men have been telling their victims they owe them something (2011:11).

Even the haunting greed of Hernán Cortés' men no longer appears as an essential human quality in this light. David Graeber (2011:333f) quotes from the diary of the expedition member Bernal Díaz del Castillo, according to which they were all weighed down by heavy debts, as huge sums had to be paid for every piece of equipment or medical supplies. Cortés prevented a revolt by ordering the most vociferous rebels to establish new colonies. These men were given control of the provinces. They created the local administrations and labour systems and set the taxes. Whereby, again, those affected had to borrow money at interest and then try to pay off these debts with labour services. In the first years of colonisation for millions of indigenous people labour systems meant being sent to the mines and pretty much directly to their death.

As another example, Graeber refers to a country where he himself lived for a long time, and whose history illustrates well both the emergence of money from debt and from the introduction of colonial taxation: Madagascar. In 1895, France invaded Madagascar, deposed the government of the then Queen Ranavalona III and declared the country a colony. As one of the first measures after the so-called "pacification", General Joseph Gallieni imposed a high capitation tax on the population of Madagascar, called "impôt moralisateur': "educational" or "moralising" tax. It was used partly to cover the costs incurred during the invasion and partly to finance the railway lines, roads, bridges, plantations, etc., i.e. the infrastructure for exploiting the land (2011:11). In other words, according to Graeber, Gallieni had money printed and then demanded to get it back via the inhabitants of the island. For the peasants it was then easiest to sell part of their harvest, but since everyone did so at the same time, given seasons and tax levy dates, the price was very low and little could be obtained for it. If food became scarce during the year, prices rose considerably. Often rice had to be bought back on credit from the same traders. As a result, the peasants, who had been able to live well until then, became hopelessly indebted (2011:57). Uprisings were brutally suppressed, but when the fought-for decolonisation was reached, it still functioned in a similar way: After independence, the Malagasy would have heard from day one that they owed France money, and that the former colonial power continued to hold on to that, and that the rest of the world thought that was fair. To the extent that when the "international community" recognises a moral problem, it is usually the assessment, says Graeber, that Madagascar is paying back the debt too slowly (2011:12).

It remains to be concluded: Ownership, labour and equivalent exchange were historically introduced by aristocrats and colonisers into societies, but under the premise that it was merely the neutral introduction of the market economy and its elements. Commons became property, and what remained as commons at the bottom of the iceberg model is still in danger of being enclosed today. This present-day robbery of commons can be observed as a consequence of the oil industry, as many indigenous people painfully experience and against which the Ogoni in Nigeria or the U'wa in Colombia, for example, are fighting. In the course of the so-called Green Economy, however, the movement *Asamblea en Defensa de la Tierra* – mainly supported by indigenous people – can also be observed fighting against wind turbines on commons in Oaxaca, Mexico.

Commons has become property, forced labour has become wage labour, and activity at the bottom of the iceberg model is constantly devalued: be it reproductive care or subsistent production. For example, the high interest rates of micro-credit to women in the Global South are just another way of cheaply siphoning off this labour. More on this also follows in chapter 4. Intrinsically motivated activity is largely confined to the family or as an unproductive hobby and is not counted as part of the economy.

All the relationships of sharing and caring in this world beyond money and the logic of exchange remain just as invisible: in families, among friends, in neighbourhoods, in black communities, etc. or spontaneous altruistic behaviour in emergency situations. Only exchange with money is visible and economically recognised as valuable and guarantees the right to a (good) life. For those who have no money, the right to participate in a (good) life is forfeited. Again, this remains profoundly interlinked with identity categories. Thus, John Locke's identitarian division continues to operate in a brutal way. But how exactly this came about will be discussed in the following part of this historical chapter.

The construction of identities in the market economy

People are part of their societal context. The following look at history, including intellectual history, is going to suggest some answers to the question of how identities are constructed. However, this can be by no means comprehensive, since discourses are far too complex for this. Only basic lines of development can be traced and presented. Discourse is always fragmented, and this aspect of fragmentation – and thus precisely resistant forces – necessarily come up short in such an outline, as in any historiography that attempts to elaborate tendencies that have become hegemonic. This is all the more regrettable because an in-depth study of aspects such as witch hunts or slavery always makes one marvel how much resistance was actually put up. This may not always become clear in the representation of historical blocs, nevertheless, it does not mean that this resistance has been ineffective; rather, it has a more invisible effect and often leads to upheavals that, in the pure consideration of hegemonic developments, mistakenly appear as granted by the insight of rulers, triggered by external events and/or exclusively caused by economic reasons.

In this study, significant attention is paid to showing how economic man became the correlate of a neoliberal mode of government, that is, the complementary counterpart. This means understanding economic man as an expression of a governmentality having developed not least as a result of securing privileges between different relations of domination, prescribing patterns of behaviour that favour some identities but ultimately "subjugate" all subjects.

Economic man and his gendered other

Those who believe that the longer an era goes back, the more oppressed women were, are mistaken. The medieval female rural population differed little from the male in physical, social and psychological terms. In addition, a subordination of women to men was mitigated by the fact that women had access to the commons.

In *Making Sex* (1990) Thomas Laqueur argues that from classical antiquity to the end of the 17th century, the idea existed that femininity was a matter of gradual deviations from a basic male type. One imagined the vagina as an internal penis and the labia as a foreskin, the uterus as corresponding to the scrotum and the ovaries to the testicles. Accordingly, women have the same organs, but in less ideal places. They are less perfect. Laqueur calls this the single-sex model. This ran through the entire period from antiquity to the 18th century: Being a man or a woman meant holding a social position and assuming a cultural role, but not being organically one or the other of two sexes.

Historians Joan Cadden, Katharine Park, among others, challenged Laqueur's identification of a unitary model of sex difference in premodern Europe, arguing for more difference in the prevailing ideas of the time (Park 2010). Yet the female as the Other of the male did not exist. According to the single-sex model, women were seen as deficient, and thus as subsidiary: In particular, where the man was absent, ill or dead, the woman could take over the male role, be it in the world of rule or in the world of peasant, artisanal and commercial work (Müller 1991:49).

In his examination of predominantly medical-philosophical texts, Laqueur works out how precisely scientific findings did not play a decisive part in the change from the single-sex model to the two-sex model, but first all results were assigned to the one, and later all results to the other model. It was the hegemonic view, which determined the conclusions drawn from scientific findings – and not vice versa.

The persecution of witches, which did not – as is often portrayed – occur en masse in the Middle Ages but only in modern times, cannot be separated from the emergence of modern society and the bourgeois male subject, its morality and its rationality. Regarding time and place, the most massive accumulations of the witch hunt often occur in connection with the social upheavals of early capitalism (Ehrenreich/English 1975:20). The contemporary theoretical justifications of the belief in witches are captivating in their linking of irrationality with formalistic reason in a virtuoso way. It was precisely men, proving in other fields to be the intellectual driving forces of humanism and pioneers of the Enlightenment, who were among the most vehement advocates of delusion (Baschwitz 1963:6f/377).

Researchers close to critical theory in particular regard this link with the burning of witches and the emergence of capitalist society as a decisive moment in the formation of the "rational" bourgeois male subject. Fundamental to this is the thesis that the mastery of nature is always accompanied by the mastery of people. The new rationality had been bought with the progressive distance of people from nature and thus also from parts of themselves. For the purpose of subjugating outer nature, inner nature had to be subjugated as well (Horkheimer/Adorno 1944:19f). As citizens, it was necessary to prove an ethical superiority over both the nobility and the dispossessed in order to morally justify economic supremacy. Adapting to such moral demands required subjects to increase their self-discipline and to regulate their lifestyles in detail. This was especially true for the rising manufactory bourgeoisie, but also for the nobility, civil servants and the military. Accordingly, the split developed right through the individuals, but in a gender-specific binary (Bovenschen 1976).

In demonising the knowledge circulating among women regarding birth, contraception and abortion, which was associated with the witch hunts, Silvia Federici sees a continuation of the expropriation of livelihoods that were shared as common goods. But her core thesis is that under the new capitalist regime, women themselves became commons, as their labour was defined as a natural resource located outside the sphere of market relations (2004:123). Increasingly, women became the representative of nature.

In the first half of the 14th century, it was still predominantly men who were the victims of these initially unusual arbitrary practices of trial and persecution. In this period, the charge was usually heresy, occurring particularly early in the south of France. A latent opposition arose against the money economy that had been developing since the 12th century, which also found expression in socio-religious and subcultural movements. In part, these were poverty movements that opposed private property and associated ways of life (Honegger 1978). Not only did many women participate in these movements – characterised by Foucault as behavioural revolts – they were often the central figures in them (Foucault 1978:284). Increasingly, it was women who were burned, first as heretics and later as witches, but what is considered the period of witch hunts did not form until the 15th century, culminating in the 16th and 17th centuries – and thus clearly in modern times.

Linked to these movements, and generally as a consequence of the theft of the commons, vagrancy became a mass movement, despite draconian punishments ranging from branding to death. Eva von Redecker sees the establishment of the property order as having succeeded only through additional forms of "phantom property," which gave the deprived people ownership-like social control power over others as compensation (2020:27). For her, this forms the basis of modern patriarchy. Thus the men deprived of the commons were participating in the modern, liberal understanding of freedom, secured by the state, guaranteeing the owners the right to do whatever they want with their own property (2020:49).

Now men also invaded the hitherto exclusively female occupied trades, took over the important functions, displaced women to auxiliary posts or altogether refused to work with women in a workshop. In the 17th century, the exclusion of women from crafts and intellectual professions was largely complete, women's guilds had disappeared in most regions (Wunder 1991).

This deprived women of their possibilities of subsistence once again and more deeply. If they vagabonded, they were in even greater danger of being burned as witches – especially if they cared more for their needs than for the new laws of enclosure. Thus Redecker brings up the example of Margaret Harkett, a widow hanged as a witch, who had picked pears in Tyburn, England, in 1585: When she was asked to return them, she angrily threw them on the ground, ergo no more pears grew. The estate manager's servant refused her yeast, whereupon the brewing equipment dried up. And the estate manager himself, who beat her when he caught her collecting wood on his land, went mad. Redecker concludes that at least this gallows was also erected to encourage the wealthy in a new skill: turning down requests for help. This self-righteous indifference to needs was to become the core of bourgeois individuality. Besides stealing, begging was made increasingly suspect (2020:72).

The witch hunt was thus of great importance for societal development. As a result rational man dominated over the woman, who was now considered closer to nature. In the newly emerging bourgeois society, this in turn was seen as a justification for denying women participation in public life.

The overall result was that pre-modern gender relations were transformed into a new form that corresponded to the relationship between sovereign owner and available resource. Increasingly, the wife's care work belonged to the husband: the claim to her property passed to him, as did later the power to decide whether she pursued paid work. In addition, there was the right to sexual access and the disposal of offspring. Spatial division as much as bourgeois morality and sexuality helped to delineate reproductive capacity and present it more and more as an attribute of gendered bodies rather than as an aspect of human activity (Redecker 2020:30f).

But even self-ownership of the male dispossessed remained broken, as they had no choice but to work for wages. Even the smallest theft offence could result in the "free workers' hands" being cut off, and repeat offenders ended up on the gallows. Redecker emphasises that self-ownership was even doubly broken, since the economic man as a bourgeois ideal was unattainable for them. All the more important the property-shaped compensatory functions of the gendered and racialised other became (Redecker 2020:70f).

Implicitly, these increasingly complementary hierarchies became the basis of the modern state order. For in the age of reason, declarations of a divine order were no longer sufficient to legitimise relations of oppression. In keeping with the zeitgeist, scientific works were produced in which supposedly biological incomparabilities were discovered and thus provided for justifying white men to be physically and mentally superior to white women on the one hand and to all the rest of humanity on the other.

Economic man and his racialised other

In his 1777 book *History of America*, Edmund Burke writes to the Scottish historian William Robertson: "Now the great map of mankind is unrolld [sic] at once; and there is no state or gradation of barbarism and no mode of refinement which we have not at the same instant under our view" (quoted in: Marshall/Williams 1982:93). John Locke, too, understood the New World as a lens through which the patterns of the first centuries in Asia and Europe could be seen. "In the beginning" he wrote in his *Treatises on Government*, "all the world was America" (Locke 1690:§49). In other words, the West had evolved from a stage similar to what had been discovered in America. Or rather: what the "white eye" was capable of seeing. The paradox of an anachronistic space associated with the Great Map of Mankind was decisive, since the unilaterally ordered time herewith – not only chronologically but also regarding space – made the Europeans the crowning glory of history, while primitive peoples still existed (McClintock 1995:159).

It was in this context that Adam Smith divided peoples according to their mode of production into hunters, herdsmen, arable farmers, and traders and craftsmen. This corresponded to the idea, prevailing as the

Great Chain of Being, that there was only one path to becoming human and civilised and that all living beings and all societies could be classified on the same scale as early or late, lower or higher. This development thesis was advocated by many, especially in the second half of the 18th century by the Scottish Enlightenment in Edinburgh and Glasgow under the influence of Adam Smith, David Hume and others. Accordingly, the anthropologist Alan Barnard calls the "hunter-gatherer society "an eighteenth-century Scottish-invention" (Barnard 2004). All civilizational advantages were seen as the result of capitalist achievements. Lord Kames put it in a nutshell: "Without private property there would be no industry, and without industry, men would remain savages forever" (Lord Kames, quoted in Marshall/Williams 1982:214).

As an illustration of the inability to deal with a different understanding of society, Stuart Hall cites Captain Cook's experiences in Tahiti in 1769. The Europeans assumed that since the indigenous people had no economic system in their sense, they had no system at all and offered gifts as a peaceful and helpful gesture to visitors whose natural superiority they instantly recognised. The Europeans therefore felt free to organise the continuous supply of such "gifts" for their own benefit. In doing so, they did not understand that the exchange of gifts was part of a highly complex but different ensemble of social practices, of practices of reciprocity, carrying meaning within a particular cultural context (Hall 1992). In conversation Captain Cook admitted that everything he had written about Tahitian society could also be misunderstandings. In contrast, the natural historians boasted that they were willing and able to examine people without prejudice (Marshall/Williams 1982:176). But by considering the indigenous people to be incapable of ownership, the colonisers saw colonial seizure of property, including capitalism and exploitation, as legitimised (Hund 2006:48).

The Great Map of Mankind and the Great Chain of Being implied European male authority over the planet – for even if Europeans were at the top of this chain of living beings, man was still the more perfect version than woman. However, both became "white" only with time. Until modern times, the skin colour of Africans had not played a systematic role in the thinking of Europeans (Jordan 1968:12). But just as the introduction of dichotomous sex bodies served as a support for new social gender roles, the introduction of social skin colour supported the myth of natural inequality on which colonialism was based (Hund 1999).

The first attempt at a systematic *division* into "races" had been made in 1684 by Francois Bernier in his essay "Nouvelle division de la terre" in the *Journal des Sçavans.* In it, he divided people according to physical characteristics, considering various possibilities such as hair, noses, lips or stature, but then mainly decided on skin colour. With Carl von Linné (1707–1778), the development towards a classification into skin colours can then be clearly traced. Considered by many to be the "father of botany" because of his systematisation of plants and animals, Linné was at the same time one of the most influential pioneers of "racial" classification. He developed this classification into a table-like overview, the systematisation of which became fundamental for the division of mankind into "races". In 1735 the Swedish naturalist describes in his Systema naturae "the European" as albescens = whitening, "the American" as rubescens = reddening and "the Asian" not as yellowing, but as fuscus = dark brownish to blackish. A good 30 years later in the 13th edition of his work *Systema naturae* (1767), Linné made skin colour the decisive basis for the different types of human beings.

Winthrop D. Jordan considers it of the utmost importance that Linné managed to refer to the Great Chain of Being and at the same time use it in a way that deprived it of its traditional meaning as a possibility of development: "If we consider the generation of animals", Linné wrote in 1754, "we find that each produces an offspring after its own kind [...] so that all living things, plants, animals, and even mankind themselves, form one chain of universal being from the beginning to the end of the world. Of all the species originally formed by the Deity, not one is destroyed."[3] Through this static understanding, the Great Chain of Being was no longer upwardly striving in all its parts, but merely a hierarchical arrangement of unchanging units, removed from temporality (Bitterli 1976:215f).

Inspired by Linné, a whole army of explorers, botanists and geographers followed the calling of subordinating the world to a global science and truth. This is where the projects of the Enlightenment and imperialism met. Colonisation made use of these systematisations: The slave trade, the plantation economy and industrialised production could not manage without these standardisations and the classifications of (human) life under a single cultural and economic maxim (McClintock 1995:34).

The idea of the Great Chain of Being, however, lost weight, as it implied, on the one hand, a hierarchy, like the single-sex model, but on the other hand the ultimate equality of people. With the typification of non-European people as backward or childlike, they appeared to be in need of help. However, this was now in contradiction with the exploitation (and sometimes genocide) in the colonial system as well as slavery, on the one hand, and the proclamation of human rights, on the other. It is no coincidence that the doctrine of polygenesis was predominantly developed and advocated in the USA and was thus regarded in Europe as the "American school" of anthropology. However, it was not least Immanuel Kant, who dismissed environmental conditions as a factor and emphasised the immutability of "races". In *Von den verschiedenen Rassen der Menschen* (1775), Kant distinguishes between different races, the basic races of which he calls white and black. Thus, parallel to the two-sex model, binarity had also arrived in the racist discourse of externalisation. But this logic of inclusion and exclusion was to become even more absolute in relation to gender and sex as well as race.

Freedom, equality, externalisation

"Freedom! Equality! Fraternity!" was the cry of emancipation during the French Revolution. Men from the French bourgeoisie in particular fought for corresponding political rights from a strong economic position. But the revolutionary mood of the Enlightenment and the slogan that all people are equal by nature made men of all classes, women, and people in the colonies believe that from now on they too would be free and equal. The optimism was partly based on the ambiguity of the word "homme": The Enlightenment demands for human freedom and equality did not of themselves exclude women or people of colour. The *Declaration of the Rights of Man and of the Citizen* of 1789 said nothing about "race" or sex and misled many into believing that the freedoms proclaimed had universal validity. In fact, women like Olympe de Gouges, in her *Déclaration des Droits de la Femme et de la citoyenne* of 1791, derived from this the same rights for women as for men.

Accordingly, the temporary president of the Legislative Assembly and advocate of extending the Declaration of the Rights of Man to women, Marquis de Condorcet, wrote that women could only be excluded from the social community if proof of a "natural difference" between men and women could be provided to justify it.[4] This is precisely what was to happen: In order to justify social differences within the framework of enlightened thinking, it was henceforth scientifically argued that human nature was not the same, but different.

On 3 November 1793, Olympe de Gouges died under the guillotine. She was followed five days later by Madame Roland, who was not specifically an advocate of women‘s rights but was a major influence in the Girondist current; she was accused, not least, of having “forgotten the virtues of her sex”. In May 1795, the National Convention decided to exclude women from its meetings, and that same week it placed Parisian women under a kind of house arrest (Schiebinger 1993:253ff). The proclamation of women’s rights had more than failed.

While the dividing lines between classes were reshuffled, the one between men and women was made all the more visible: Alleged biological differences between male and female bodies were produced in a variety of contexts to justify this exclusion. The question about “equality” was answered by anatomists. Two biological sexes were invented in order to give social genders a new basis. Sex replaced gender. A framework was created, in the first place, within which the natural and the social were clearly separated (Laqueur 1990:173/177). This offered a biologically based incomparability of the sexes and thus the possibility of explaining how – already in the state of nature and before the existence of social relations – women were subordinate to men. Regardless of the argument in detail, in the end women could be considered excluded from the new civil society for reasons inherent in their “nature”, inhabiting bodies preventing them from making “reasonable” use of political freedom or assuming civic responsibility, since they were characterised by irrational qualities (Laqueur 1990:224). Consequently, the social contract could then only be concluded between (white) men.

Women thus emerged from the French Revolution with fewer rights and privileges than they had previously enjoyed under the Ancien Régime. Before the convocation of the Estates General in 1789, a few privileged women had the right to vote, mainly heads of religious orders as well as some nobles and widows. While men’s opportunities had already expanded and women’s had diminished since the beginning of the modern era, in the early 19th century the opportunities of European women were worse than ever before (Anderson/Zinsser 1988:20). All women – regardless of age, class and skin colour – were denied civil rights.

Accordingly, in “racial science” women were hardly the object of comparisons: Anatomists in 18th century Europe were obsessed with black males, Schiebinger argued, as the dominant sex of an allegedly inferior “race”, and white females as the allegedly inferior sex of the dominant “race”. More than women of African origin, these two groups provoked the male ruling classes of Europe with their call for equal rights and political participation (Schiebinger 1993:209).

Ultimately, through biologisation the sexes thus also became increasingly socially charged, and the cultural ideals of the two sexes became increasingly polarised. Femininity was defined as belonging in the home, masculinity was formed not least through the daily competition of emerging capitalism. This ideology was particularly directed at the women of the bourgeoisie, as it painted a positive picture of the newly domesticated woman. The caring woman – turned towards the private sphere – emerged as a foil for the rational man turned towards the public sphere (Schiebinger 1993:65).

Like the bourgeois man, the bourgeois woman constituted herself in distinction. The more the bourgeois family took shape, the more it defined itself through demarcations: from other cultures, from the servants, from the neighbourhood, and finally within itself with a separation between parents and children, and between boys and girls (Honegger 1978:119). The dichotomous structure, fundamental to the societal order, also implied a hierarchisation, since "the Other" always represents the excluded, the suppressed of the first "pure" part – so that in the two-sex model the hierarchisation of the single-sex model was implicitly preserved. At the same time, it was a form of patriarchal domination of property that enabled a section of the dispossessed in Europe as well as the white settlers in the colonies to enjoy the arbitrariness of the owner, as has already been argued.

In revolutionary France after 1789, even more obviously, a short period of successes in the emancipation of people of colour was then truncated by increased oppression. The call for "Liberty, Equality, Fraternity" did not go unheard in the French colonies. But it required the slave uprising in Santo Domingo (now Haiti), which, beginning in 1791 – despite an army of 18,000 soldiers initially sent from France, after years of bloody fight – ultimately led to full equality for all. But under Napoléon Bonaparte, as early as 1802, slavery and the criterion of skin colour were reintroduced in the French colonies, according to the rule that anyone who was not completely white was black. The only exception – after renewed fierce fighting – was Santo Domingo: On 1 January 1804, the first black republic could be officially proclaimed. Jean-Jacques Dessalines took the lead by snatching the white from the French flag.

While many Americans hoped to infect other nations with the "epidemical liberty" (Reverend Ezra Stiles) after their War of Independence, and Thomas Jefferson still considered their own influence on other nations' liberation struggles an "animating thought" in 1790, the successful revolution in the colony of Santo Domingo suddenly turned their own slaves into potential insurgents. In 1797, Jefferson warned, "the revolutionary storm, now sweeping the globe, will be upon us, and happy if we make timely provision to give it an easy passage over our land" (quoted from Jordan 1968:386). Their own revolution had taken on a life of its own, had not only found imitation in Europe, as expected, but with the uprising in Santo Domingo showed that it was coming back to America – and as a danger to those who had started it. Here again the dilemma arose between the ideal of equal and thus free individuals on the one hand, and the justification of slavery on the other. The way out here was also to argue that blacks were not equal to whites, and thus, as with sex, to refer to a biological difference (Jordan 1968:91).

Yet slavery did not run along racial lines from the beginning. The first 20 black slaves, traded for food at a Dutch ship in 1619 by the governor in Virginia, were granted nearly the same rights as the white unfree labourers. For a large part of the European population came as unfree labourers, as emigrants who could not pay otherwise for their passage by ship to the New World and were therefore in debt bondage. If the indentured servants had already been able to conclude a contract before their departure, the redemptioners had to rely on the offers made upon their arrival. As a rule, the period of service was between four and seven years; for blacks usually longer than for whites, but then as well released to freedom. If an African was freed, he too could own slaves (Finzsch/Horton/Horton 1999:54ff).

But the charging of skin colour with meaning took place earlier here than in the academic European discourse for a very obvious reason: Africans were quicker to identify when fleeing because of their skin colour, while Europeans blended in more easily. Whiteness thus became an assurance of superiority even for the dispossessed, and was equated more and more unambiguously with being free, blackness more and more unambiguously with being slave – a self-reinforcing process. In 1661, lifelong slavery was legalised. In 1662, a law stipulated that the status of joint children of Africans and Europeans should depend on the status of the mother, thus turning the principle of English common law on its head. From 1669, a slave owner who killed a person he had enslaved went unpunished. In 1670, African Americans and Native Americans were prohibited from buying whites. Skin colour increasingly determined social position (see Finzsch/Horton/Horton

1999:58ff; Jordan 1968:81). In 1691, the term "white" found its way into Virginia's laws to designate people of European descent.

So again dominium went as absolute power over things together with the right to kill. In this context, Redecker quotes the scene from Fyodor Dostoyevsky's *Crime and Punishment* in which a person – beating his horse to death in agony – comments "It is my property!" (in German: "Es ist ja mein Eigentum!"). Almost simultaneously with stipulating someone as black whoever was not completely white, the "despotism" of the owners was explicitly formulated as a right in the Code Napoléon: In addition to rights of use and transfer, the owner also possessed the *ius abutendi*, the right to abuse his property. And again, more than 100 years after John Locke's apparently legitimising property, the promise of freedom as the right to do with one's belongings as one pleases was thus enshrined in law (Redecker 2020:32f/24f).

In general, in the sense of discourse theory, the connections shown here must not be reduced to a simple cause–effect causality, even if this may sometimes appear so in hindsight. Discourses and resulting practices emerge as contingent outcomes of a multitude of variables. In this way, slavery cemented the difference of others. This was not only due to the interests of the slave owners, but was done in a circular argument: The white soldiers maintained colonial oppression, while the white researchers examined the manufactured inferiority "objectively" as a seemingly natural biological phenomenon. The researcher, who constantly encountered his objects in the subjugated role of the colonial labour force, inevitably saw little more than their inferiority (Terkessidis 1998:94). Just as hegemony is never just ideology, but is always turned into reality to some extent. At the same time, however, hegemonic discourses do not form independently of what proves suitable for legitimising and securing hegemonic structures. And here the effect was twofold: directly towards the racist and sexist oppressed, and towards the classist oppressed as compensation. However, this is perhaps less to be seen as inclusion by transfer of privilege than as shared conviction by a critical mass of men and a critical mass of whites.

Nevertheless, the more the discourse boiled down to the dichotomy between "black" and "white" and "the black" became "the other", the easier it could be instrumentalized against a solidary attitude of the lower classes in Europe. In the following 19th century, whiteness became an invitation card to feel part of the ruling colonial (nation) states in Europe and the free working class in the USA. The puzzle of why the ownership of nothing but one's skin should appear to be an attractive freedom is solved abruptly if the contrast is modern slavery (Redecker 2020:28ff). The inclusion of workers operated through the exclusion of others: in Europe with the help of national borders, in the USA through the laws on discrimination against anyone considered non-white.

Thus the call for "Liberty, Equality, Fraternity" implied a process of complex exclusions at the same time. The skin colour of slaves became charged with social significance, and physique took on a new, urgent signification. Just as slavery was opposed to freedom, the colour of the slaves had to become the opposite of the colour of the free: "we and our slaves are not different", Jordan quotes a slaveholder, "but opposite; our badges of distinction are black and white" (quoted from Jordan 1968:513).

The newly defined characteristics of the newly defined blacks, just like those attributed to women, were constructed as the antithesis of adult masculinity. Neither women nor people of colour could become citizens or economic subjects in this logic – especially since the former legitimised themselves through the latter.

Economic man and his internal externalisations

Economic theory and its theorists are both an expression of societal discourses and formative for them. Adam Smith is regarded as the intellectual father of economic theory as well as of liberal economics and thus laid the decisive foundation for the emergence of homo economicus. Even though the term did not appear until 150 years later, he is credited with having recognised and presented the economic importance and moral value of self-interest. The expression according to which everyone who strives for his own profit is guided by an "invisible hand" and thus contributes to national prosperity (1776:349), made a career for itself. The basis for this is the ability to decide rationally what serves one's own benefit.

However, Smith implicitly assumed that only white bourgeois males were capable of making rational decisions. As already indicated, Smith saw the development of economies, and thus of humanity, proceeding in four stages with each of them still existing. Only one paragraph in the originally multi-volume main work deals explicitly with women. In it, young women are not trusted to decide for themselves what they wanted to learn, let alone become. In Smith's *Theory of Moral Sentiments* (1759) it can be read even more clearly that his statements are tailored to men. For example, it is said that the lack of restraint in the expression of feelings is the reason that one half of humanity makes poor company for the other. As of then, this double ethic runs through Smith's entire work. Thus he was also the first to make the dichotomous assumption of perfect egoism in the market and perfect altruism at home. Edith Kuiper compares Adam Smith's concept of gender with that of Sir William Petty, who lived a hundred years earlier. She notes a crucial difference between the two: Smith "not only ascribes different tasks to women and men as Petty did, but also different characteristics and features to both sexes to a point where "the fair sex" almost becomes another species" (Kuiper 2001:93).

However, Adam Smith does not describe masculinity in general, but how civic identity re-articulates masculine identity. It is the internalised civilisation that enables to control emotions. Among all misfortunes, to Smith the loss of reason seems by far the most terrible. But "the poor wretch, who is in it, laughs and sings perhaps, and is altogether insensible of his own misery" (Smith 1759:30). Contrary to Smith's usual criterion, according to which compassion is based on visualising what we ourselves would feel in the same situation, here, however, only the (personified) observing "humanity" feels the "anguish". Accordingly, for Adam Smith, non-rational human beings are excluded from being human.

That Smith also excludes people of the lower class from his ethical considerations becomes equally clear when he writes that a man of low status cannot be distinguished by qualities that serve a man of higher status to gain authority – be it appearance, manner or conduct. This also explains why, according to Smith, mere poverty inspires little mercy. Only the fall from wealth into poverty rarely fails to arouse the most serious pity; such a person is usually helped. Although suddenly impoverished, a citizen does not lose his civic identity. Last but not least, it is probably the internalised discourse of how a citizen should behave that makes it possible to articulate suffering in a way that is heard in bourgeois society. The citizen learns to be able to express himself in any situation in a "reasonable" way.

Here, the inner struggle is essential for Smith. Page after page Smith elaborates on both the "Jurisdiction of the man within" as well as on the "Jurisdiction of the man without" (Smith 1759:159ff). The Creator of nature, who still remains the supreme controlling authority, has appointed man as his governor on earth to supervise the conduct of his brothers – this represents the jurisdiction of "man without". But a far higher tribunal is the tribunal of one's own conscience – the jurisdiction of the "man within", that assumed an impartial and well-informed observer in the breast of man. It is obvious that "I" (and thus citizens) am divided into two persons in such cases: the examiner and judge on the one hand, and the examined and acting on the other (Smith 1759:150).

When reading today, it is important to remember that Smith was not simply describing his contemporary reality, but that his descriptions became a model for an entire class. At the time of publication in 1759, the bourgeoisie had not yet become hegemonic vis-à-vis the nobility and did not yet represent such a distinguished identity as Smith would like. Instead, partly due to the later success of Smith's *Wealth of Nations*, in the end both books contributed significantly not only to the formation of this identity, but also to the marginalisation and exclusion of women, the underclass and non-European people. Smith's theory on moral sentiments and the concept of identity it presents has a whole range of implications both for the subject defined as white, male and bourgeois, and for the "Others" constructed in sexist, racist and classist distinction to it. It is only one form of masculinity he considers ideal, and thus hegemonic.

Smith's remarks fit well into Michel Foucault's analysis of the disciplinary society and the techniques of the self. Smith elaborates how much this subject, elevated to the status of an ideal, is oriented towards what his peers will think of him: always subject to control by society. Edith Kuiper, referring to Smith's remarks on self-control, states: "In the end, it is no longer the balance between humanity and self-command which constitutes the perfect human being but the identification with the impartial spectator and self-command" (Kuiper 2001:106).

Smith's remarks are later implicit in the effect of Jeremy Bentham's 1787 design of a prison form, the Panopticon: In this, the individual cells are arranged in a circle around an observation tower allowing clear view of all cells. Here, at any time, each of the inmates can be observed by the guard and every aspect of their behaviour can be controlled without the inmates being able to know when this is the case: The observation is not to be noticed, but the inmates are to be aware of it. Precisely because the individual inmate cannot know when they are observed from the tower, they must assume that they are monitored at all times and behave accordingly. There is no cruel punishment for non-compliance – Bentham sees no benefit in such measures – but release depends on whether the inmate's behaviour is to the satisfaction of the guards. Thus, constant self-monitoring becomes a duty out of self-interest. This is the magic of the Panopticon.

At the same time, Bentham is the most important founder of utilitarianism, according to which people always choose between pain and pleasure. This combination makes it doubly interesting, for the Panopticon is seen by Foucault as a symbol of the internalisation of control in bourgeois society, and thus as an expression of a technology of power characteristic of modern societies as a whole: no longer directed at the body, but at the "soul" – which, however, acts on the body, thus making the soul the "prison of the body" and the correlate of a power technique (Foucault 1975:42/129). In other words: Disciplining is internalised as a technology of the self. This subtle form of regulation – the "microphysics of power" – is not a diminished but, on the contrary, an expanded exercise of power that encompasses every aspect of daily life. While traditional power worked through visibility and fear, disciplinary power worked precisely through its invisibility. This reveals the limitations of the democratic freedom of the sovereign subject in Western thought: Freedom is based on the disciplining of soul and body.

Thus, with the rise of industrialisation, the spread of disciplinary techniques in factories, schools, military barracks, psychiatry and families was not only about increasing economic profit by shaping an adaptable and controllable workforce for factory work. According to Foucault, government is not as a technique applied by the state, but he conceives the state itself as a technique of control, as a dynamic form and historical fixation of societal power relations. This is the reason why Adam Smith's theory became so essential to the reality of society. This principle of government required the "freedom" of the governed and the "rational" use of this freedom. In this, the liberal art of government is oriented towards the model of the market, assuming natural equilibria (on the labour market, etc.). It was no longer a matter of judging these practices as good or bad in terms of a moral principle, but as true or false; a "new regime of truth" (Foucault 1979:37) emerged.

Accordingly, an important transformation of the techniques of government took place as of the middle of the 19th century, with the state taking on a completely new meaning: no longer partisan and potentially despotic, but seemingly standing neutrally above and outside society with its conflicts. It thus became the regulatory instance of political antagonisms (Foucault 1979:29; Lemke 1997). This is where civil society developed and thus was a decisive field for the negotiation of interests and power relations, as analysed by Gramsci.

At the same time, rationality is increasingly seen as entrepreneurial rationality. Foucault calls this a kind of permanent economic tribunal (Foucault 1979:342). At the same time, a "democratised panoptism" emerges (Bröckling 2000:152): In place of the all-seeing observer on the one hand and the objects of observation, which are extremely limited in their own possibilities of observation, on the other hand, there is a non-hierarchical model of reciprocal visibility in which everyone is at the same time the observer of all others and the observed by all others. Like Bentham's architecture of control, this aims at a concatenation of increased fitness and deepened submission.

The human being who shows a lack of initiative, of adaptability, dynamism, mobility and flexibility apparently "objectively" proves their inability to be a free and rational subject. However, the ability to behave according to business criteria such as effectiveness and efficiency in one's own life plan is increasingly regarded as the basis of a society consisting of autonomous individuals. Ulrich Bröckling summarises this:

> Whoever has success deserves it; whoever has none has done something wrong. All mistakes, in turn, basically boil down to the one mistake of not (sufficiently) orienting oneself to the market. Empowerment and humiliation go hand in hand. If everyone can achieve what they want, those who fall by the wayside have not wanted it any better (and consequently deserve their fate).
>
> *(Bröckling 2000:162; translation F.H.)*

The emphasis on freedom in the economy is thus not only an auspicious one; the individually different use of freedom is also seen as the reason for the wealth of some and the poverty of others. The existence of poverty thus seems to be a constant reminder of where the wrong use of freedom can lead. However, since the danger of being split off as void can affect anyone, this freedom ultimately oppresses everyone – including the CEO, and even the capital owner of today takes credit from the image of the apparently highly successful use of this freedom. But this also threatens them with societal failure.

In his book *The Corrosion of Character* (1998), Richard Sennett shows how modern capitalism transforms responsibility for the other into the "teamwork-we" of a flat community and thus into indifference. The other could always be replaced at will. In this way, their uniqueness in the sense of Lévinas, who defines ethics as the relationship to the other, is lost. At the same time, the self-worth of the subject, which according to Lévinas develops primarily in relation to the other, dissolves in the exchange relationship. In order not to be replaced oneself, the ideal image must be maintained externally.

Since, according to Eva von Redecker, the decision about the value of the goods, in a way, is left to the things themselves,

> the domination that exploitation establishes over us, is separating the valuable from the worthless, anonymously and indirectly. It is a 'factural' rule, not a personal relationship of dependence. The fact that we perceive value as a natural property of a thing makes it extremely difficult to see through this domination. You don't even know that you are being dominated. Or even if you vaguely sense it, you don't know the source – every conspiracy theory, but especially modern anti-Semitism, feeds on this impenetrability. The material domination consists in our powerlessness vis-à-vis things stemming from capitalist exploitation. A comprehensive picture of it, however, must shed light not only on its value but also on its rejects.
>
> *(2020:55f; translation F.H.)*

Economic man and his externalisations of today

The possibility of economic success for women/people of colour is now taken for granted. Economic man has become the role model for (almost) everyone. The image of the rational, flexible and efficient individual dominates the discourse to such an extent that women/people of colour also orient themselves towards this ideal. Indeed, unequal employment and income opportunities are always worthy of newspaper articles or individual studies, but the image of far-reaching equality of opportunity is widespread in society. Yet, because economic man has emerged in interaction with the construction of the white, male bourgeois, it remains easier for members of this identity to succeed. This does not mean that people of this identity are always the winners. It is about the privileging of a certain form of white masculinity, and not necessarily of white men. This privileging is understood as an expression of a governmentality that has emerged between various relations of domination, prescribing patterns of behaviour that favour some identities but ultimately subjugates all.

Today's diversity is thus reminiscent of the diversity of Barbie dolls: Even in those models that are supposed to stand for diversity, a striking sameness prevails in their features which correspond to the features of success and employability; in short, economic man. It is obvious that this is difficult for people from de-privileged class positions. But if the façade and performance are perfect, skin colour and gender have become less important in this logic.

In this respect, Kornelia Hauser (1996) speaks of a "new one-sex model". Likewise, one could speak of a new Great Chain of Being. As the hegemonic ideal is interwoven with the construction of masculinity and whiteness, women/people of colour are considered the more imperfect version, as with the historical one-sex model. With regard to women, Susanne Schunter-Kleemann formulates:

> It is obvious that in this noble contest, which is recommended to the female sex, the losers are likely to be determined even prior to the competition. And it is neither due to a lack of will to achieve, nor to the lack of risk appetite on the part of many women, but has to do with 'location disadvantages'.
>
> *(1997:135)*

In her study *Capital Culture. Gender at Work in the City*, Linda McDowell quotes a director of the North Bank, summarising this aspect as follows: "It's not going to work. I'll never be a man as well as a man is" (1997:156).

Economic man, just as with Marx's figure of the doubly free worker (as first free from slavery and second free from means of subsistence) includes liberation from reproductive labour. This is why we should actually speak of the triply free worker (Brenssell/Habermann 2001). Not least because of this necessary liberation from reproductive work for women who want to make a career, neoliberalism leads to what Brigitte Young (1999) summarises as a "re-construction of 'class, gender and race'". The dividing lines between gender, class and race are blending in historically new formations – and at the same time follow the old familiar structures of oppression. Thus, the old bourgeois model of mistress and maid is found again in today's form, when working and socially privileged, predominantly white women buy themselves out of domestic work. Here, firstly, through the transfer to informalised employment domestic work again remains invisible. Secondly, the role of a new form of "maid" usually falls to a non-white woman, often from a country on the periphery – sometimes under threat of deportation, but at least without an occupational alternative, since training is not recognised or work permits are not granted.

Yet these conditions, which force migrants to sell their labour cheaply, are not simply a given, but in this case they are part of a struggle for (the maintenance of) white privilege. Trade union policy in industrialised countries is still characterised by the active support or even demand of corresponding laws. Bridget Anderson (2000), who empirically studied many such employment relationships, emphasises that wage differences alone cannot account for the fact of predominantly ethnicised women being employed as domestic workers. It is also racist stereotypes, albeit often linked to insecure residence status, that construct some women as specifically suited for domestic work. This leads to an increasing racialisation of domestic work.

All in all, one must also speak of a continuity of inequality. While the impression of the laws of economics working as an impartial force, making class, race and gender inequality seem a normal to inevitable outcome in the pursuit of maximum wealth, there is an everyday entanglement of sex, race and class in the struggles for hegemony. Here, privileges and identities are reproduced – never identically, but in continuities. Less subject-related than the catchphrase "doing gender", Randolph Persaud formulates: "Race works in constituting these systems of inside/outside. Race is thus a verb, a kind of action, active in the making of social phenomena" (Persaud 2003:133).

With her thesis that the theft of the commons was partially compensated for by property-shaped social power of control over others, Eva von Redecker provides a further explanation for these simultaneously existing violent racisms and sexisms. In other words: The reification of social relations along the lines of property allowed the dispossessed white male to become property rulers as well, and to be allowed to live the promise of radical freedom, namely in a partial sphere to do as one pleases (2020:25ff). In *Patriarchy and Capital* Maria Mies formulates that a man who is married to a housewife also receives his "colony" through patriarchal marriage, specifically in the form of sexuality and care work (1986:186). In continuation of her thesis, Eva von Redecker argues that the emancipation movements achieve self-ownership for some, which appears to others as amputation. Like a pain in an empty place, where there used to be a limb that could be controlled, the void claims to domination persisted (2020:13f). Instead of material domination, "phantom property" spread.

In other words, since men often continue to regard their wives as their own, they feel unjustly dispossessed by a separation, for example. And white phantom property manifests itself in seeing racialised persons as a potential thing or a potential thief, and thus putting them in the vicinity of available property (Redecker 2020:36). Where these persons are, what they do and what they are entitled to is thus considered a matter for their white counterpart. Even after the prohibition of slavery, black lives were therefore considered expendable, and even after the abolition of patriarchal marriage, the female sex was considered prey. Phantom property is thus a basic building block of modern identities. So someone can have phantom property – or be it (2020:14/34f).

Redecker argues that capitalism is doubly divisive. The first cut, which determines its order, is set by property and runs between the material ruler and the object. The second cut divides the object of material domination, because the intention of utilisation draws a dividing line between commodity and waste, between value and the void (2020:14). That the same can be said about the subject itself was already discussed in the last section.

Economic man as a hegemonic model has another serious consequence: Within it, people not only recognise how they supposedly function themselves deep inside, but also what they have to expect from their fellow human beings. They become more cautious and reckon with the fact that other people are also only pursuing their own interests. "Whoever had fully grasped this doctrine, could no longer be disappointed when he finds nothing but egoistic benefit-calculations in a person by whom he hoped to be loved – for the hope of being loved itself has become clear to him as a deception" (Manstetten 2002:120; translation F.H.).

The historic development of economics and with it the development of economic man, as well as the development of identity categories, show that this was less a conscious process of obfuscation than the development of a theory that became more and more consistent because those who developed it developed more and more in this direction themselves, as it seemed to correspond to their interests or their privileges.

Notes

1 Quoted from: Wolfgang Hardtwig (1997) *Genossenschaft, Sekte, Verein in Deutschland. Vom Spätmittelalter bis zur Französischen Revolution*, Vol.1, Munich: C.H. Beck, 111.

2 Martin Luther (1525) Wider die mordischen und reubischen Rotten der Pawren; https://daten.digitale-sammlungen.de/0002/bsb00027508/images/index.html?id=00027508&groesser=&fip=qrssdaseayafsdryztseayaqrsyztseayafsdren&no=5&seite=7.
3 From the Introduction to *Museum Regis Adolphi Friderici*, Upsaliae 1754; quoted from: Jordan 1968:221f.
4 Marie-Jean-Antoine-Nicolas de Caritat, Marquis de Condorcet (1790) *Sur l 'admission des femmes au droit de cité*; quoted from: Schiebinger 1993:208.

References

Anderson, Bonnie S./Zinsser, Judith P. (1988) *Eine eigene Geschichte. Frauen in Europa, Vol.1: Verschüttete Spuren. Frühgeschichte bis 18. Jahrhundert*, Frankfurt/M.: Fischer, 1995.

Anderson, Bridget (2000) *Doing the Dirty Work? The Global Politics of Domestic Labour*, London/New York: Zedbooks.

Barnard, Alan (2004) "Hunting-and-Gathering Society: an Eighteenth-Century Scottish invention", in: Alan Barnard (ed.), *Hunter-Gatherers in History, Archaeology and Anthropology*, Oxford/New York: Routledge, 31–44.

Baschwitz, Kurt (1963) *Hexen und Hexenprozesse. Die Geschichte eines Massenwahns*, München: Gondrom, 1966.

Bitterli, Urs (1976) *Die 'Wilden' und die 'Zivilisierten'. Die europäisch-überseeische Begegnung*, Munich: dtv, 1982.

Bovenschen, Silvia (1976) "Die aktuelle Hexe, die historische Hexe und der Hexenmythos", in: Claudia Opitz (ed.), *Der Hexenstreit. Frauen in der frühneuzeitlichen Hexenverfolgung*, Freiburg/Basel/Vienna: Herder, 1995, 36–98.

Brown, Elizabeth A.R. (1974) "The Tyranny of a Construct: Feudalism and Historians of Medieval Europe", *The American Historical Review* 79(4): 1063–1088.

Brenssell, Ariane/Habermann, Friederike (2001) *Geschlechterverhältnisse. Eine zentrale Dimension neoliberaler Hegemonie*, Berlin: rls.

Bröckling, Ulrich (2000) "Totale Mobilmachung. Menschenführung im Qualitäts- und Selbstmanagement", in: Ulrich Bröckling/Susanne Krasmann/Thomas Lemke (eds), *Gouvernementalität der Gegenwart – Studien zur Ökonomisierung des Sozialen*, Frankfurt/M.: Suhrkamp, 131–167.

Ehrenreich, Barbara/English, Deirdre (1975) "*Hexenkunst und Medizin im Mittelalter*", in: Claudia Opitz (ed.), *Der Hexenstreit. Frauen in der frühneuzeitlichen Hexenverfolgung*, Freiburg/Basel/Vienna: Herder, 1995, 18–35.

Federici, Silvia (2004) *Caliban and the Witch. Women, the Body and Primitive Accumulation*, Brooklyn/NY: Autonomedia; quoted from *Caliban und die Hexe. Frauen, der Körper und die ursprüngliche Akkumulation*, Vienna: Mandelbaum, 2017.

Finzsch, Norbert/Horton, James O./Horton, Lois E. (1999) *Von Benin nach Baltimore. Die Geschichte der African Americans*, Hamburg: Hamburger Edition.

Foucault, Michel (1975) *Discipline and Punish. The Birth of the Prison*, New York: Vintage Books, 1979; quoted from *Überwachen und Strafen. Die Geburt des Gefängnisses*, Frankfurt/M.: Suhrkamp, 1997.

Foucault, Michel (1978) *Sicherheit, Territorium, Bevölkerung. Geschichte der Gouvernementalität I*, Frankfurt/M.: Suhrkamp, 2004.

Foucault, Michel (1979) *Die Geburt der Biopolitik. Geschichte der Gouvernementalität II*, Frankfurt/M.: Suhrkamp, 2004.

Graeber, David (2011) *Debt. The First 5000 Years*, New York: Melville House; quoted from *Schulden. Die ersten 5000 Jahre*, Stuttgart: Klett-Cotta, 2012.

Gronemeyer, Reimer (1991a) "Einleitung", in: Reimer Gronemeyer, *Der faule (N-word). Vom weißen Kreuzzug gegen den schwarzen Müßiggang*, Reinbek: rororo, 7–12.

Gronemeyer, Reimer (1991b) "Vom weißen Kreuzzug gegen den schwarzen Müßiggang", in: Reimer Gronemeyer, *Der faule (N-word). Vom weißen Kreuzzug gegen den schwarzen Müßiggang*, Reinbek:rororo, 13–79.

Hall, Stuart (1992) "The West and the Rest", in: *Formations of Modernity*, ed. Stuart Hall/Bram Gieben, Milton Keynes: Polity Press/The Open University, 275–320.

Hauser, Kornelia (1996) "Die Kulturisierung der Politik. 'Anti-Political-Correctness' als Deutungskämpfe gegen den Feminismus", *Aus Politik und Zeitgeschichte. Beilage zur Wochenzeitung Das Parlament*, B 21–22/96, 15–21.

Honegger, Claudia (1978) "Die Hexen der Neuzeit. Analysen zur anderen Seite der okzidentalen Rationalisierung", in: Claudia Honegger (ed.), *Die Hexen der Neuzeit. Studien zur Sozialgeschichte eines kulturellen Deutungsmusters*, Frankfurt/M.: Suhrkamp, 21–151.

Horkheimer, Max/Adorno, Theodor W. (1944) *Dialektik der Aufklärung. Philosophische Fragmente*, Frankfurt/M., 1998; translated as: *Dialectic of Enlightenment. Philosophical Fragments*, New York: Herder and Herder, 1972.

Hund, Wulf D. (1999) *Rassismus. Die soziale Konstruktion natürlicher Ungleichheit*, Münster: Westfälisches Dampfboot.

Hund, Wulf D. (2006) *Negative Vergesellschaftung. Dimensionen der Rassismusanalyse*, Münster: Westfälisches Dampfboot.

Jordan, Winthrop D. (1968) *White Over Black. American Attitudes Toward the Negro 1550–1812*, North Carolina: Chapel Hill.

Klein, Thomas (1975) "Die Folgen des Bauernkrieges von 1525. Thesen und Antithesen zu einem vernachlässigten Thema". *Hessisches Jahrbuch für Landesgeschichte* 25, 65–116.

Kuiper, Edith (2001) *The Most Valuable of all Capital. A Gender Reading of Economic Texts*, Amsterdam: Tinbergen Institutef.

Laqueur, Thomas (1990) *Making Sex. Body and Gender from the Greeks to Freud*, Cambridge, MA: Harvard University Press; quoted from: *Auf den Leib geschrieben. Die Inszenierung der Geschlechter von der Antike bis Freud*, Frankfurt/M./New York: Campus, 1992.

Lemke, Thomas (1997) *Eine Kritik der politischen Vernunft. Foucaults Analyse der modernen Gouvernementalität*, Berlin/Hamburg: Argument.
Locke, John (1690) *Two Treatises on Government*, London: Awnsham Churchill.
Luxemburg, Rosa (1925) *Einführung in die Nationalökonomie*, edited by Paul Levi [without place]: [without publisher].
Manstetten, Reiner (2002) *Das Menschenbild der Ökonomie. Der homo oeconomicus und die Anthropologie von Adam Smith*, Freiburg/Munich: Alber.
Marshall, P.J./Williams, Glyndwr (1982) *The Great Map of Mankind. British Perceptions of the World in the Age of Enlightenment*, London/Melbourne/Toronto: Dent.
McClintock, Anne (1995) *Imperial Leather: Race, Gender and Sexuality in the Colonial Conquest*, New York/London: Routledge.
McDowell, Linda (1997) *Capital Culture. Gender at Work in the City*, Oxford: Blackwell.
Mies, Maria (1986) *Patriarchy and Accumulation on a World Scale*, London: Zed Books.
Million, Alison (2018) "The Forest Charter and the Scribe: Remembering a History of Disafforestation and of How Magna Carta Got Its Name", *Legal Information Management* 18(1), 4–9.
Moore, Jason W. (2015) *Capitalism in the Web of Life. Ecology and the Accumulation of Capital*, London/New York: Verso; quoted from *Kapitalismus im Lebensnetz. Ökologie und die Akkumulation des Kapitals*, Berlin: Matthes & Seitz, 2020.
Müller, Maria E. (1991) "Naturwesen Mann. Zur Dialektik von Herrschaft und Knechtschaft in Ehelehren der Frühen Neuzeit", in: Heide Wunder/Christina Vanja (eds.), *Wandel der Geschlechterbeziehungen zu Beginn der Neuzeit*, Frankfurt/M.: Suhrkamp, 1993, 43–68.
Park, Katherine (2010) "Cadden, Laqueur, and the 'One-Sex Body'", *Medieval Feminist Forum* 46(1), 96–100.
Persaud, Randolph B. (2003) "Power, Production and Racialization in Global Labor Recruitment and Supply", in: Isabella Bakker/Stephen Gill (eds.), *Power, Production and Social Reproduction. Human In/Security in the Global Political Economy*, Hampshire/New York: Palgrave Macmillan, 124–145.
Redecker, Eva von (2020) *Revolution für das Leben. Philosophie der neuen Protestformen*, Frankfurt/M.: S.Fischer.
Reynolds, Susan (1994) *Fiefs and Vassals. The Medieval Evidence Reinterpreted*, Oxford: Clarendon Press.
Schiebinger, Londa (1993) *Am Busen der Natur. Erkenntnis und Geschlecht in den Anfängen der Wissenschaft*, Stuttgart: Klett-Cotta, 1995.
Schunter-Kleemann, Susanne (1997) "*Die Modernisierung patriarchaler Gewaltverhältnisse*", in: Regina Stötzel (ed.), *Ungleichheit als Projekt. Globalisierung – Standort – Neoliberalismus*, Marburg: BdWi, 1998, 125–142.
Sennett, Richard (1998) *The Corrosion of Character. The Personal Consequences of Work in the New Capitalism*, New York: W.W.Norton & Co.

Smith, Adam (1776) *An Inquiry into the Nature and Causes of the Wealth of Nations*, London: Strahan&Cadell; quoted from *Wohlstand der Nationen*, Munich: dtv, 1990.
Smith, Adam (1759) *Theory of Moral Sentiments*, Edinburgh; quoted from *Theorie der ethischen Gefühle*, Frankfurt/M.: Georg Kurt Schauer, 1949.
Terkessidis, Mark (1998) *Psychologie des Rassismus*, Opladen/Wiesbaden: VS.
Wood, Ellen Meiksin (2002) *The Origin of Capitalism: The Longer View*, London/New York: Verso; quoted from *Der Ursprung des Kapitalismus. Eine Spurensuche*, Hamburg: Laika, 2015.
Wunder, Heide (1991) "Überlegungen zum Wandel der Geschlechterbeziehungen im 15. und 16. Jahrhundert aus sozialgeschichtlicher Sicht", in: Heide Wunder/Christina Vanja (eds), *Wandel der Geschlechterbeziehungen zu Beginn der Neuzeit*, Frankfurt/M.: Suhrkamp, 1993, 12–26.
Young, Brigitte (1999) "Die Herrin und die Magd. Globalisierung und die Re-Konstruktion von 'class, gender and race'", *Widerspruch. Beiträge zur sozialistischen Politik*38/2000, 47–59.

4

ANY MARKET RELIES ON EXPLOITATION AND (PRODUCES) EXTERNALISATION

If, among the reasons why an emancipatory society cannot be based on the market, the following does not deal in detail with the capitalist surplus value exploitation of wage workers, it is because its critique has been made countless times – which emphasises its centrality. But the focus here is not only on capitalism, but on pure market mechanisms. It is shown that a good life for all is not possible within the coercions of the market. For the market is always operating in the ways described by the following mechanisms – and each of these mechanisms has counter-emancipatory effects.

Nevertheless, Marx's analysis of exploitation should be taken as the starting point: Surplus value results from the fact that living labour adds more value to the product than is contained in the equivalent value of the wage. It is not much different from the purchase of an ox by a small farmer; here too the ox creates more value than it consumes. As differently as an ox can be kept, so wages also can be barely enough for basic survival or for a good living, or, for example, through post-colonial dividends in the Global North at the expense of the Global South, luxuriant. Regardless of this, if the purchase of the ox did not pay off for the farmer or the hiring of the worker did not pay off for the employer, there would be no employment relationship. Exploitation is what Marx calls the skimming off of surplus value. The difference between the farmer and the employer is that the ox would hardly create surplus value without direct coercion, and thus

DOI: 10.4324/9781003373360-4

the living labour of a human being remains necessary. The employer, however, could have inherited the money or borrowed it from the bank, and leave all the work to managers, and would still get richer in every round of production (assuming economic efficiency). The fact that hardly anyone still corresponds to this image of the non-working capitalist does not change anything economically, but merely points to the internalisation of the work ethic, even among those who do not need it financially.

From the perspective of commodity exchange, however, such a work contract is the contract between two equals, both determined by free will. Marx ironically calls this "a very Eden of the innate rights of man. There alone rule Freedom, Equality, Property and Bentham". He continues:

> Freedom, because both buyer and seller of a commodity, say of labour-power, are constrained only by their own free will. They contract as free agents, and the agreement they come to, is but the form in which they give legal expression to their common will. Equality, because each enters into relation with the other, as with a simple owner of commodities, and they exchange equivalent for equivalent. Property, because each disposes only of what is his own. And Bentham, because each looks only to himself.[1]

Marx did not describe this perspective as wrong. Yet, while it is not wrong, it is also not right. There is another perspective to the same circumstance as Marx explains:

> On leaving this sphere of simple circulation or of exchange of commodities, which furnishes the 'Free-trader Vulgaris' with his views and ideas, and with the standard by which he judges a society based on capital and wages, we think we can perceive a change in the physiognomy of our dramatis personae. He, who before was the money-owner, now strides in front as capitalist; the possessor of labour-power follows as his labourer. The one with an air of importance, smirking, intent on business; the other, timid and holding back, like one who is bringing his own hide to market and has nothing to expect but – a hiding.

In 1983 the Marxist and feminist Nancy Hartsock added this idea: "When we follow the worker home from the factory, we again witness a transformation of the dramatis personae. The worker, just a moment ago walking behind, shy and reluctant, now walks upright, followed by a third person who carries the shopping, the baby and the nappies" (Hartsock 1983:234). From the point of view of the average Fordist worker, this also appeared to be a fair division of labour. However, not contractually based, not as part of the public sphere, but of the private. Public and private represents another binary division by the market economy. What is private was considered a non-political sphere until the women's movement. Since this division of labour was basically justified by women's biological functions, it was naturalised.

But let's move on: If we follow the housewife – or even better, ourselves today – into the supermarket, workers on the coffee plantations in Central America, kept like serfs, appear in the background. If we go to the flower shop, we meet the employees from Colombia poisoned by pesticides. We might hurry past the carpet shop and the clothing discounters afterwards and – with a deeper reach into the pocket – try to console ourself with a shirt made of pure cotton: But here we meet thousands of left-behind families from cotton production in India, whose male breadwinners took their own lives in desperation due to their indebtedness.

What are the economic reasons behind the correlations shown here? One often reads formulations according to which "capitalism" is the cause. Here we take a closer look and it becomeslear that it is the market economy. Just to emphasise: there is no such thing as a market economy without capitalism. The growth compulsion described below quickly leads every market economy to employ workers and thus to the exploitation of surplus value. However, the following considerations are about understanding why the market always structurally works against emancipation, and why an emancipatory society based on any kind of a market is not possible.

Structural coercion to exploitation and externalisation

The decisive reason why the conditions depicted in the "iceberg model" occur in every market economy is simple: The market is based on the fact that, all other things being equal, the cheaper variant wins and the more expensive one disappears from the market. But the cheaper option can be the one that exploits nature in an unbothered way, takes over care activities unnoticed and exploits labour the most. This is what the much-vaunted competition is all about: It is a structural compulsion for companies to exploit people, animals and nature. This means that the logic of money and the market not only seduces people into making money instead of preserving NATURE, but it also structurally enforces destructive exploitation.

This structural compulsion to exploit does not only exist towards the externalised elements in a supply chain. However, here the noble values of civil society apply less or not at all. This is precisely what enormously facilitates exploitation, and that is why there is not only the urge to exploit the externalised in a particularly crude form, but also to further and further externalisations.

As mentioned in the introduction, it was Rosa Luxemburg who first pointed this out. In doing so, she also criticised Marx: In his model of "simple reproduction", the class of capitalists consumes all the surplus value, nothing remains. This corresponds to a static economy. An expansion of reproduction therefore means a partial addition of surplus value from previous production as an investment. The surplus value is not consumed, but reinvested and thus new constant and variable capital is bought and thus production is expanded. This is the value level that Marx captures – he neglects the factual level, according to Luxemburg. On this level, there is a need for more means of production and more labour, as well as more food ("since the workers cannot live on money"). In addition, in order to be able to sell the increased mass of products and thus to realise them again in the form of money as capital, an expanded market was needed (1913:12ff). In this way, Marx implicitly contradicted his own schema. For to write that the inner contradiction seeks to balance itself out by expanding the outer field of production is incompatible with his assumption of the exclusive capitalist mode of production. The question of where the additional resources, labour and demand come from remains unresolved. Luxemburg's conclusion: While the history of capitalism is characterised by periodic expansion by leaps and bounds, Marx's scheme excludes precisely this. In reality, on the other hand, there has never been a self-sufficient capitalist society (Luxemburg 1913:270).

As central to this, Luxemburg analyses the urge of individual capital to cheapen the elements (1913:279). In today's business management terms, this is "squeezing". Evi Hartmann, a professor of supply chain management, writes: "Squeezing is pushing the supplier's price down so hard and so long that, like a squeezed lemon, he can't do it any more, is finally sent into insolvency and replaced by a new one." If he complains about those who have ruined him, he will hear: "But we ourselves are under immense price pressure!" (Hartmann 2016:19f). And this is exactly what the bankrupt entrepreneur had told their workers. Hartmann's book which translates as "*How Many Slaves Do You Keep*?" revolves around the fact that for the average consumption of one person in Germany, 60 people have to work under slave-like conditions. Hartmann also mentions, under today's conditions it is scientifically a point of contention where forced labour ends and wage labour begins. Even where it is legally possible, the working conditions do not always differ.

However, hardly any manager tries to change this, says the supply chain expert. Contrary to the would-be-pleasers' image as doers and soloists, hardly anyone in middle management dares to even fetch copy paper from the office supplies store without six signatures. But at least they can get signatures. Not for morally driven concerns. The supervisor at the latest reacts again with: "Believe me: I also feel sorry for the suppliers! But I have a duty to the supervisory board. And to the shareholders! I would love to! But my hands are tied!" (Hartmann 2016:25f).

The final argument of "I'd love to, but my hands are tied" is, also according to Hartmann, that whoever buys wants cheap. *The Knowing-Doing Gap* (2000) is what Harvard professors Jeffrey Pfeffer and Robert I. Sutton call the discrepancy, also on the side of the consumers, between knowledge and morality on the one hand and action on the other. But here, too, this gap is not primarily a question of character, but owed to the fact that other things have to be paid for. And even where this was not the reason, resorting to the cheaper option is nothing more than an internalisation of what our economy, and thus our society, reproduces itself on: always keeping an eye on one's own advantage.

"Human labour is not, of course, intrinsically 'cheap' or 'expensive'", as Spivak (1988:275) puts it. Making women/people of colour as well as animals NATURE enables cheapness. This is impressively shown in detail by Patel/Moore in their book *A History of the World in Seven Cheap Things* (2017). In it, they illustrate both historically and for today how people, nature, care etc. have become and continue to become "cheap ingredients" for profit. Their list of seven items, as they themselves note, is not to be understood as the only or complete one; in 2015 Moore had still written of the Cheap Four (food, energy, raw materials and labour), here care, lives and money have been added. Either way, for the law of value, it is merely a matter of bundles of non-capitalised labour/energy (or, in the case of cheap money, the further reduced access to it).

The feminist critique from which the Iceberg model stems emphasises the aspect (which is also taken into account by Patel/Moore) that the labour capacity of "cheap" people which does not have to be paid with the costs necessary for their (re)production, lies in the mostly unpaid reproductive activity of (traditionally, and still mostly) women. First of all, it is about everything that enables the worker to be available again the next day, but also the housewife herself or the person working in subsistence agriculture or the double-burdened reproductive worker who herself also works for wages, etc. Beyond that, it is about all that is necessary so that the next generation is available as a labour force. Christel Neusüß summed this up in her 1985 work *Die Kopfgeburten der Arbeiterbewegung oder Die Genossin Luxemburg bringt alles durcheinander* [The Head-births of the Workers' Movement or Comrade Luxemburg Upsets Everything]: "My mother is not selling my labour power, that's the catch" (1985:259).

As in Hartsock's picture, the watershed between the valued and the unvalued, at least as long as people are concerned, takes the form of a Great Chain of Production: the further back, the greater the proportion under water. If the top manager perhaps has to do nothing below the surface of the water, the saleswoman has to smile and the outpatient nurse in many cases conceals the fact that she did not complete the home visit in ten minutes. It is no coincidence that the care workers in richer countries often come from relatively poorer countries, since it is not possible to make a good living in the same location of the work place, but only elsewhere (the latter aspects are dealt with in more detail in the next section).

Further down the chain, the consequence is wage levels that would not even be sufficient without subsistence work. For example, when the wages of African miners only make a living possible together with vegetables subsistently grown by female relatives. Since the vegetables are not sold or bought before they are eaten, they do not exist for the statistics. This is one of the many ways in which the subsistence activities, rendered invisible in this system, are incorporated in the exploitation process.[2] At the end of the Great Chain of Production we then find the slave-like working conditions where people are only used and exploited.

Once again, it is not only capitalists who profit from this, but basically everyone who can now buy smartphones cheaper. Who is located where in this Great Chain of Production is also rooted in the struggle for hegemony and emancipation. It is the struggle to get into the hegemonic bloc and as high up there as possible. This is not only an individual struggle, but is based on and reconstructs identity categories.

But behind this works the law of value, which requires structural inequality. This life activity articulated outside of commodity production, but with it, Moore calls socially necessary unpaid work (2015a:463). He sifted through various estimates of the share of unpaid work and comes to the conclusion: for those of humans (still predominantly women), the share varies between 70 and 80 per cent of the world's gross national product. If animals and other "ecosystem services" are included, the estimates go up to 250 per cent (2015a:103). But seen from today, if the bees die and the flowers have to be pollinated by hand or by machine in the presence of following generations – how should that be evaluated? Or what about the suffering of human and non-human beings associated with species extinction?

It is not really possible to value what has been destroyed, because, strictly speaking, NATURE cannot be quantified in the same way as what is commodified as there is no assessment basis. For value is not an intrinsic property, but only arises through market logic. Demands to pay the "true costs" of resource use call for an impossibility, Moore argues, because that would mean not only asking capital to pay its bills, but calling for the abolition of capitalism (2015a:224f).

He speaks of "accumulation by appropriation" as "those extra-economic processes that identify, secure, and channel unpaid work outside the commodity system into the circuit of capital" (Moore 2015b:2). At the core of appropiation, Moore emphasises, are not (post-)colonial power structures or neoliberal privatisations, but how capitalism lowers its basic costs of production (Moore 2015a:226). At the same time, usability is not simply there.

> Scientific, cartographic, and botanical revolutions, broadly conceived, are good examples. During the rise of capitalism, for example, a new way of seeing – and imagining – the world took shape. The world could be comprehended from outside rather than from within. It was of course a partial perspective, treating the specifically capitalist ordering of the world as 'natural'.
>
> *(Moore 2015b:2)*

Reproduction within the logic of money, on the other hand, is expensive, and the longer and the more a hitherto non-capitalist sphere is drawn into it, the more expensive it becomes. With time, workers also begin not to put up with everything. Although in many cases "capital" succeeds in suppressing trade unions and repressing strikes, the tendency is for wages to rise. This is precisely the essential reason why capital keeps sweeping around the globe in search of un(der)paid labor instead of simply letting its share grow above water. This is not a linear process. Many areas of the world have been more firmly tied into wage-labour relations before and have been (partially) spat out again. If the situation for the now "proletarianised" people, still deprived of their subsistence livelihoods, is desolate enough to once again be vigorously exploited, capital may come back.

Squeezing is reinforced by two independent effects of the market. One relates to care activities, the other to exchange relations between the Global North and the Global South.

Where equitable exchange leads to exploition

This structural compulsion to exploitation is supported by the different productivity rates that emerge with market logic. Where no additional NATURE can be attached to, those who are already integrated into the re/production process are exploited more profoundly: Digging for resources reaches deeper into the soil, using even more toxic pesticides intervenes even more deeply in the existing agrarian conditions, labour processes are made even more exhaustive, ever cheaper migrant workers are sought ever more systematically in the East or South.

It is said that health care is becoming more and more expensive. In Great Britain alone, there are 300 to 500 deaths per week in accident and emergency units due to the desolate supply situation.[3] However, it is only getting more expensive in comparison, as it is becoming cheaper and cheaper to produce industrial products. The IT revolution has exponential potential to streamline the manufacture of industrial goods. People, on the other hand, need time to grow up or get healthy. Here two "logics of time" collide. Frigga Haug (1996) speaks of the overall socially "time-saving logic" (*Zeitsparlogik*) on the one hand, which results from the fact that whoever produces faster can produce cheaper. And on the other hand, for the care activities, there is a "time-expenditure logic" (*Zeitverausgabungslogik*) – because the child cannot simply be put to bed and to sleep much faster. For this reason, the exchange relationship between productive and reproductive activities deteriorates more and more at the expense of the latter.

The poor exchange ratio of reproductive versus productive activities on the market will therefore tend to pay care workers less than industrial workers, at least in the skilled professions. Therefore, care work tends to be left to the underprivileged identity categories. Historically and today, it can be observed that these jobs are not only almost universally assigned to certain groups of people, but their identity categories are often first constructed as particularly suitable for them. While until the middle of the 20th century there was scholarly talk about the "monotony resistance of women", today the image of the "patient Polish woman" does the rounds at cocktail parties where people chat about Eastern European caregivers for their parents. In other words, these categories are (re)constructed at the same time.

Where the state withdraws from the care sector, the so-called "double privatisation" occurs. On the one hand, this can mean that private enterprises become providers instead of state institutions. However, only the wealthy can afford this. On the other hand, there is a shift into the (invisible) private sphere, i.e. care must be provided within the family (or, more rarely, the circle of friends) in addition to employment and other existing obligations. As an intermediate form, care is provided by informal employment relationships, taking advantage of the different productivity and price levels between countries, which are also generated by the different possibilities for rationalisation. This creates what Arlie Russel Hochschild (2000) calls the "global care chain", which is also referred to as the care drain: Women from poorer countries migrate to richer countries in order to perform care work there, which partly compensates for the care deficit there, but withdraws the care potential from the countries of the Global South.

The cost pressure in the paid care sector has consequences for both care-receivers and care-givers. For residents of old people's homes, it can mean having to beg to go to the toilet.[4] And while in productive areas a "Taylorist work organisation", i.e. the dissection of a work process into the smallest units, is considered to have been largely overcome and autonomous activities are supposed to characterise today's work organisation, the reverse is true for care-givers. The same applies to external surveillance in an obvious form. In an interview with Beatrice Müller, an outpatient geriatric nurse describes the GPS, to be carried at all times to monitor performance, as a kind of anklet (Müller 2016:160).

Müller illustrates the aspect of Taylorisation with a variation in wording by changing an original care instruction for the performance of "washing" a body in such a way that the body becomes a car, the bed becomes a garage, etc. This works smoothly. What remains unnamed in the instructions is the unpredictable (such as body parts that unexpectedly become dirty, which, since their cleaning was not purchased, should not be remedied) as well as the relational (Müller 2016:129f). For touching cannot be reduced to the purely mechanical execution of an assistance; it is characterised by a complexity that makes it significant. This complexity is reflected in the resonance between care giver and care receiver. Accordingly, caregivers feel torn between the two logics of time. A geriatric nurse describes what it means:

> "When I have a patient, he is on their list for about ten minutes with injections and putting on stockings, so roughly, and I go there. But I know, as the person who always goes there, that he has dementia, that he first has to walk down the stairs from upstairs, that he then has to say hello to his (pet) on the right, because he always does that when he walks past there, 15 minutes have gone by. I want to say hello to him, too. I don't want to say, 'We're going downstairs right now because we have to do this,' exactly, but I first say, 'Hello. How was your day?' That's already two minutes, I find that very limited, then I say: 'We're going to walk down the stairs and we can still continue talking', because I still have to see where I'm going to stay in my schedule […] Most of the time, to be honest, I click it off earlier, so those ten minutes I have, I click it off, and if he wants to talk to his (pet) for five more minutes, then he can talk to his (pet) for five minutes, I'm not going to take that away from him for God's sake, I'll drive faster through the city for that."
>
> *(quoted from Müller 2016:156)*

As in this case, Müller's interviews illustrate how nurses repeatedly try to subvert the regulations for the benefit of their patients. But there are narrow limits to the attempt to enable resonance. The result is "simply a totally guilty conscience" (quoted from Müller 2016:166).

Without the distinction between "increasingly rationalisable" and "hardly rationalisable", the distinction between productive and reproductive activities becomes invalid. For if it is care to put a child to bed – why should it not be care to build the bed? If it is care to administer food to a sick person – why should it not be care to grow the food? Just like preparing the vegetables for the mine worker after they have been grown in the garden in a subsistent way. This non-separability was also an aspect of the ecofeminist analysis called housewifisation.

That rationalisability is the true dividing line is also clear from the fact that there is a very similar connection between industrialised countries and those specialising in raw materials, tourism or food. Their production, too, can hardly be rationalised. And if it is, it is of little use to the producers. Here, too, the cause is not an unequal exchange relationship enforced by (post-)colonial dependencies and military power, as has been strongly suggested in the theory of dependency – even though such global power relations undoubtedly play a major role and are closely related to the point under scrutiny here. But here, too, the exchange that appears to be fair according to market logic already leads to ever worsening terms of trade.

In 1949, the economist Hans Wolfgang Singer, who fled from Germany to Great Britain in 1933, published a refutation of the classical theory of comparative cost advantage, which goes back to David Ricardo, according to which two unequally developed countries each benefit from foreign trade with one another. Inspired by this, in 1950 the Argentinian development economist Raúl Prebisch published a continuation of this thinking; today the result is known as the Prebisch–Singer thesis.

Starting from industrialised countries on the one hand and developing countries on the other as two large economic areas, trade with each other results in the latter becoming increasingly worse off. Empirically, Prebisch proved this by looking at Great Britain's foreign trade figures between 1876 and 1947. The Prebisch–Singer thesis also proves this in theory. In the following, this is traced with cocoa and televisions.

Since cocoa is not particularly different from cocoa, there is strong competitive pressure, which is why more cocoa basically only leads to falling prices. And even if it succeeded and people in cocoa production now earned more, due to different income elasticities of demand for primary goods (relatively independent of the level of income) and for industrial goods (clearly increasing) this rising income would mainly result in increased purchases of industrial goods, and drive economic growth in the industrialised countries. Not in the cocoa-producing countries.

Adam Smith was already aware of the effects of different productivity developments. However, Smith does not initially describe this connection using the example of nations, but rather the early capitalist development of cities on the one hand and the countryside on the other. Similar to industrialised and developing countries, significantly more valuable goods could be produced in urban crafts with the same labour input than in the peasant economy, and here, too, the different advances in productivity became apparent. In the direct exchange of their goods, urban producers thus structurally found themselves increasingly at an advantage. This made it possible for urban crafts to externalise the competitive pressure on the rural population by depressing the prices for the purchase of goods necessary for production. In the long run, according to Smith, these advantages stabilised and increased: "A city might in this manner grow up to great wealth and splendour, while not only the country in its neighbourhood, but all those to which it traded, were in poverty and wretchedness" (Smith 1776:303).

Already then, different productivity developments went hand in hand with isolation: The town people closed themselves off internally and externally by protecting themselves against external competition. According to Stephan Lessenich, this is still the case today, despite all the talk of free trade. For this is the only way to enjoy wealth at the expense of others. Only in this way is it clear who belongs to the privileged and who to the exploited. Only the isolation on the basis of externalisation enabling exploitation allowed the "Keep it up!" to become the overall societal project of the Global North (Lessenich 2016:152). In this way, divergent exchange relations also develop internationally, and have nothing to do with equal work or equal suffering. Oliver Schlaudt formulates that the Global South is "no longer exploited in the sense which held for the epoch of colonialism. Today, the countries of the periphery and those at the centre are interconnected via the international market instead of being exploited through sheer violence" (2023:282).

The rural population in the industrialised countries, however, gained access to the area above the water, raising up to civil society, not least through colonisation. This struggle for privilege seems to correspond to the reason for growth that I learned in my economics studies: The pie has to get bigger so that everyone can have more. But there is a more fundamental growth imperative of the market economy. And it is not including everyone.

The market forces growth and increasing exploitation of nature

Not only as individuals are we forced by market logic to do or not to do something. Market logic forces the economy to grow. The growth spiral has to keep spiralling upwards, because capitalism cannot stand still. If it doesn't grow, it goes into crisis. Standing still would only be possible if no company wanted to gain sales markets – but it is precisely this competition that constitutes the market mechanism. The market functions by way of all companies always trying to conquer sales markets. This is not an optional decision. Whoever can use *economies of scale* increases competitiveness, i.e. whoever grows and thus can save labour. Those who do not follow suit risk losing their own sales markets to competing companies. Under the rule of competition, as Luxemburg described it, in the struggle for a place on the sales market the most important weapon of the individual capitalist is producing cheaper goods. All permanent methods of reducing the production costs of commodities, however, amount to an expansion of production. For the individual capitalist, the impossibility of keeping pace with this general movement means dropping out of the competitive struggle, economic death (1913:9/11).

In my studies, I also learned that it is easy if the economy grows because then the rich don't have to share. Critics of interest rates point to the compulsion to grow that results from the repayment of interest. These are correct points of view. But there is an even more fundamental compulsion to grow. In talks I describe this with the simple example of chair production.

The initial situation is that a person can produce and sell one chair per day – let's pretend it's me. If a competitor comes along and not only does the same, but manages to produce two chairs a day, then *ceteris paribus* (the economic mode of saying "all else held constant"), my competitor can sell the chairs at half the price. Since my chairs are now too expensive, I go bankrupt unless I manage to produce just as much and as quickly. In that case, I work and earn just as much as before, only the world has twice as many chairs. An increase in productivity, which in itself is welcome, becomes a compulsion and an end in itself due to the pressure to compete.

Since this is a very contrived example, in the real world it takes 23 years to double total economic output at the rate of growth of three per cent that the OECD countries are still striving for and that has also been achieved worldwide (with downs and ups due to the Covid-19 pandemic). Since it is exponential growth, it takes only another 14 years to triple, the next time only 10 years. And so on and on, faster and faster. The tenfold increase is reached after 78 years. Of course, it then takes another 23 years to double it again, so that a twenty-fold increase in the original output is achieved after 101 years.

Since this is only a value-based consideration, the situation is actually worse. By increasing productivity, more and more past labour (and thus also knowledge and inventions) is stored in constant capital, which can be used in the new production periods without having to be done again. So more efficiency does not mean more surplus value, but on the contrary less. What Marx understood as a tendential fall in the rate of profit is based on an exponential increase in the volume of material in production, which, however, does not correspond to an increase in abstract labour. Fewer people produce more: more calories, more shoes, more cars, more stuff, this is how Moore describes the logic of labour productivity, whereby more and more extra-human nature is attached to every single quantum of societally necessary labour time (2015a:94).

There is no "decoupled" growth, as the myth of "green" "qualitative" growth would have us believe. Only a relative decoupling of growth and increasing resource consumption, but not an absolute one. It has been empirically proven many times that growth is always linked to an absolute increase in resource consumption.[5] And where it is claimed otherwise, it is at the national level without taking outsourced production into account. This is called the *rich country illusion effect.* But even beyond empirical evidence or Marxist analysis, according to rebound expert Tilman Santarius, the connection between efficiency and growth becomes clear in the fact that the goal to become more efficient is a commonplace for economists and the daily bread for managers (2012:132). But not in order to put the saved capital under the pillow; efficiency is the engine of growth, which allows capital to be turned over for profit even faster. The positive correlation between increased efficiency and economic growth is the be-all and end-all of economics.

This results in an ominous correlation: Our exponential economic growth consumes more resources, and produces more waste and toxins. If we manage to limit CO_2 emissions, it will be at the expense of other raw materials or environmental destruction. And everything is happening faster and faster. This is the great acceleration of resource depletion on the one hand and pollution on the other, be it as earth system trends or as socio-economic trends. Raj Patel summarises this exponential acceleration into one graph "of bad things".[6] On the occasion of a press conference in 2021, where the German Chancellor Angela Merkel explained exponential growth to the population on the occasion of the pandemic, Christian Stöcker, co-author of a book on the Great Acceleration, suggested that she should do the same with reference to economic growth. Again with the addition that action must be taken.[7]

This actual growth compulsion brings with it a second reason that has been almost universally present in global economic policy since the financial crisis of 2008 at the latest. Even without societal economic growth, there are increases in productivity in individual areas. This reduces (national) surplus value, and without additional growth, labour is released. As a result, there is less (national) income, which means that people can buy less, which further reduces demand, which means less production, which in turn releases labour, and so on. It is the multiplier effect that Keynesian economic policy aims at, only reversed as negative growth or downward spiral with all too easily uncontrollable consequences for the economic and financial system.

So if in 2020, due to the lockdown, people were not allowed to leave their homes and therefore did not buy new shoes and other things, then this negative spiral is immediately set in motion. Not least because of this, during the pandemic hundreds of billions of euros, dollars, etc. were pumped into the world market to ensure the stabilisation of the global economy. And this did not just happen in the financial crisis of 2008. Also in the intervening years, when the respective central banks made additional euros, US dollars, yen, reminbi and, to a lesser extent, pounds available on a large scale, complementing each other and taking turns; in 2017, it amounted to 180 billion per month, at that time by the EU and Japan.

Advocates of socio-ecological transformation often argue that growth would go hand in hand with less resource consumption if there were a switch from environmentally harmful to environmentally friendly processes, which in turn would increase wages and gross domestic product. After all, economic growth means an increase in the monetary value of all goods and services in a country. By now, word has spread that this also increases when cars cause accidents, and increases even more when they cause serious hospitalisations in the process. But when the state shifts subsidies from the car industry to the care sector for socio-ecological reasons, economic growth falls, because care and other reproductive sectors yield less profit than productive sectors. Especially since more money for hospitals should not be used to care for more accident victims with the same poor care capacity. Cost-intensive care does increase GDP, because money is spent, but only in the short term, since it is not an investment with a profit perspective. Just as little as is reforesting rainforests or fishing plastic from the sea. It is the opposite of the growth-driving efficiency imperative. So arguing with growth in this sense obscures the fact that it is actually a degrowth policy, since the shift will make the economy grow relatively less.

As a way for the state not to have to choose between ecological restructuring on the one hand and intensive care workers, plastic collection etc. on the other, the post-Keynesian Modern Monetary Theory (MMT) has been discussed in recent years. Basically, this is the already existing practice of money making described above, only this time with a view to a Green New Deal, i.e. investments in green growth areas. Up to now, it has predominantly been considered a privilege of the USA to be able to multiply its own currency on a large scale without risky inflation levels, since the US dollar is the most important reserve and trade currency. MMT representatives see this possibility for other stable states as well. In this way, money is not redeployed, but added, and the economy grows.

This is not wrong, but basically it only applies to the former colonial powers, whose currencies, albeit compared to the dollar to a much lesser extent, can also serve as reserve currencies. Other countries would immediately lose massive monetary stability. This is why there is a great danger, which is not so much new as old: the selling off of the Global South by newly created money in the Global North. Just as money was printed by the colonial powers in the past and had to be paid back through taxes on cottages and the like, the available resources would likewise be sold today. This is the more so since the debt crises, which for the first time reached unprecedented heights with the Latin American debt crisis in the 1980s, continue to ensure that year after year a multiple of money is "paid back". The widely publicised debt relief system plays its part here. The debt system ensures control of the economic policy of the affected countries through the guidelines of the International Monetary Fund. An expansionary monetary policy of an indebted country in the Global South would simply not be permitted.

The fact that increased labour productivity requires more and more extra-human nature reverses the common thinking about capitalist development, as Moore rightly observes. Capitalism does not grow in order to expand the field of commodification as such, but it expands in order to shift the balance of world accumulation towards appropriation. For if there is increased capitalisation of production, the rate of profit decreases and symptoms of capitalist stagnation appear, such as growing inequality, financialisation, etc.

But it is becoming increasingly difficult to get extra-human nature to render its gifts cheaply. Oil sands, fracking, just to mention a few, are examples showing that for the extended exploitation of new resources more and more destruction of nature is accepted. Moore even sees a rise in the cost of food production and resource extraction since 2003 possibly meaning a potentially epochal collapse of the strategies and relations having sustained capital accumulation over the last five centuries (2015a:8). So far, this rise has been postponed by technological revolutions and a decline in the rate of profit through measures such as increasing money supply or, before that, the shift towards financialisation. This has ensured capitalism's survival. But these spatio-temporal forces drive capital to an accelerated extraction of NATURE.

However, this is at the expense of the web of relationships needed to maintain the increasing material output. There is more at stake here than just increasing production costs through resource depletion. The economic process always also includes the production of non-recyclable waste. Already in the 1970s, economist Nicholas Georgescu-Roegen wrote that every new Cadillac reduces the life chances of future generations. Not least, the incompatibility of nature as a tap of resources and nature as a waste and toxic dump are growing into immediate obstacles to the restoration of unpaid NATURE (Moore 2015a:424). To an ever greater extent, this also means the destabilisation of those conditions that have ensured the stability of the biosphere and biological health for millennia. This corresponds to what Rob Nixon (2011) calls "slow violence". Climate change is the most debated example of this. However, it is not the only one. The devastation caused by extractivism, the poisoning and littering of land and sea, all this and much more should be mentioned here, and thus, as a consequence, especially the extinction of species. The accumulation of the limits set for capital in the web of life threatens to turn surplus value into a negative value. Or to put it another way: The conversion into a negative value is a question of time (Moore 2015a:467).

Paradoxically, we cannot simply slow down or even stop the process, let alone reverse it. On the contrary, the market economy forces us to turn the wheel of slow violence ever faster. However, the market economy has always been violent. Even in its golden age.

Artificial scarcity: exclusion of sufficient resources

Not even material prosperity for all is possible through the market exploitation of nature. Without abundance or under-utilisation on the one hand and scarcity on the other, no market economy can function – regardless of how much of a resource is actually available. Even non-economists are usually familiar with the graph that forms the core of economics: The horizontal axis depicts the quantity of a good, the vertical its price. The supply curve runs from the bottom left to the top right and means: the higher the price, the more of this product is offered. The demand curve runs from top left to bottom right and says: the lower the price, the more people can afford the product. Where the two lines meet, the equilibrium price is formed. So to the right above this point the discarded good, e.g. food, can be found.

The line below on the left represents all those products that have not been produced, although there may be people who would like to do so but cannot afford it under today's competitive conditions. For example, people who would like to work in organic farming. In other words, due to the system, a large part of society cannot afford not only consumer goods, but also activities: Activities that we find necessary and/or in which we could find our respective personal fulfilment.

One thing is essential to understand here: Before the introduction of money, which partly arose in foreign trade but was mostly motivated by colonisation, there was no society where individuals exchanged goods in this way. "For centuries now, explorers have been trying to find this fabled land of barter – none with success", writes David Graeber (2011:35). Conversely, it can be said: Different cultures had very different forms of economy. Only barter in the intended economic sense as equivalent exchange did not occur.

Even without money there is exchange logic – that is the myth. Even Yanis Varoufakis elaborates on this in his book *Talking to My Daughter About the Economy: or, How Capitalism Works – and How it Fails.* "Before money was invented, exchanges were direct: a banana would be exchanged directly for an apple, or maybe two apples [...] The first time one of our ancestors offered to trade a banana for some other fruit, a market exchange of sorts was in the air" (2013:10). Wherever this land of bananas and apples may have been, it would only be a market (for that is precisely what exchange with exchange logic is) either in the unlikely event if a banana already held the same exchange value as one or two apples. But in the case of two, and the other person has only one apple, then the person with the banana would break its fruit into two. And would add: "Whether I eat the other part myself or throw it in the dirt is none of your business, because your apple is worth less than my banana". And even if the one with the banana had so many of them that they were already rotting away, they wouldn't give any of them away if the other person didn't have apples or anything else to offer. And that other person would starve to death. That is exchange logic. Exchange logic – and thus every market – artificially creates scarcity.

To our ancestors, that would have seemed absurd. Not so to us. Because we find it normal that food goes where the money is – and is largely thrown away there – nearly a billion people are starving. Market economy kills. Tens of thousands every day. In history, there have always been isolated famines due to drought or other events, but hunger as a permanent condition came into the world through market economy, as Mike Davis points out in his work *Late Victorian Holocaust. El Niño Famines and the Making of the Third World*: "Millions died, not outside the 'modern world system', but in the very process of being forcibly incorporated into its economic and political structures" (2000:9). Nothing has fundamentally changed in this respect. Of course, people also die through colonial power relations, capitalism's exploitation of surplus value, food speculation, etc. But all these are additional. The logic of exchange is sufficient enough.

The principle of artificial scarcity applies to all goods. Evi Hartmann sums it up: "The market is the god of the saturated, not of people with empty stomachs" (2016:30). Because if you have nothing to trade in, you get nothing. Nor does anyone who has nothing to give but their own life, when life is so abundant that umpteen thousands of them a day are extinguished by our way of doing business. As if it were a matter of overproduction.

Davis also analyses the creation of our contemporary image of "the starving". He illustrates his book with photos of these severely undernourished people, which mark the production of the "Third World". As every form of domination must emphasise the boundaries between dominant and dominated identities, "the starving" is one such constructed identity made real. Liberalism thus not only produced tens of millions of deaths; it also produced victims who were not worth mourning. Davis emphasises this with regard to the Indian Viceroy Lord Lytton, who was decisively behind this policy: "Lytton, to be fair, probably believed that he was in any case balancing budgets against lives that were already doomed or devalued of any civilised human quality" (2001:32).

This identity construction, while generating paternalistic pity, unconsciously contributes to the fact that these subjects are no longer recognised as human beings in the sense of equals. It is well known that malnourished children cannot fully develop their intelligence or other abilities. In this way, generations of people are constructed who seem doomed to poverty from the start. They are "unproductive", "inefficient" and subject to global competition for resources – having landed there in a seemingly natural way from the supposed starting point of equal opportunities for all. This too is a form of externalisation. And this constitutes a major aspect of the persistence of global hunger. Or who could imagine a global policy that causes the death of tens of thousands of people from the Global North every day and is pursued for decades? With at best half-hearted attempts to remedy this "collateral damage"?

But again, the principle of artificial scarcity applies to all goods. And even as the god of the saturated, it can be quite demanding. The premise of pricing is scarcity, and all pricing creates artificial scarcity and thus people not getting what would satisfy their needs, be they consumptive or productive. And thus the market creates pressure to exploit oneself in order to be entitled to goods.

Any market produces fear and alienation and relies on structural hatred

The following reasons why the market and the logic of exchange are contrary to an emancipatory society are on an individual and interpersonal level, respectively, and arise from the situation of what such a person with a pile of bananas would say to the person without an apple, according to economics: "Work for me! So you shall receive your just reward!"

In order to be entitled to the banana, I have to utilise myself. So I could offer to massage the person with the bananas. But then I have to do it better than any other person who also offers to do it in exchange for bananas. That's why already children can't sleep before exams: Pressure to perform. In their song *Haben oder Sein (To Have Or To Be)*, the musicians *Jens Böttcher & das Orchester des himmlischen Friedens* sing about "Leistungskriegsverletzte": the wounded of the performance war.

The workers' existence or, for many of us an easier identification, the labourers' is reduced to a commodity, with which they share all the uncertainties of sale. In this way, human qualities have themselves become commodities. What this means for the individual is explained by Dieter Duhm in *Angst im Kapitalismus* [Anxiety in Capitalism]: There is no property, no merit principle and thus no competitive society without fear. His book is also interesting because he wrote it in

1972, and thus at the height of the welfare state, still untouched by the pressures of neoliberalism. But Duhm sees a permanent source of anxiety in the performance principle. The achievement principle inevitably leads to fear of failure, and the more deeply the achievement principle becomes embedded in all activities and relationships, the more fear of failure becomes a basic component of life as a whole (1972:55ff).

Moreover, money as an external motivation destroys inner motivation, which concerns the desire to do something as well as helpfulness and a sense of responsibility. And this happens straight away. In the literature on employee motivation, this is called "The Gummy Bear Effect". In the underlying experiment, children are drawing pictures, e.g. fairies, sea monsters and pirate ships with many details. When it is then announced that for every picture there is a gummy bear, the pictures gradually become more volatile until the kids shift to mass production, churning out simple images with increasing speed and sloppiness. Then, when they are told there are no more gummy bears, they all put down their crayons and have forgotten that they originally drew out of enthusiasm. This effect has been confirmed in numerous experiments – be it with one-and-a-half-year-old children who originally help of their own accord and then stop as soon as rewards are introduced, or with adolescents who become lazy, or with adults who lose any sense of responsibility towards others.[8] Whereas the reverse process, the restoration of desire, helpfulness and sense of responsibility through the removal of the money does not succeed.

We have to exploit ourselves so that we get money, and in the process, as we have already seen, become more and more productive. This creates stress. In 1998, in his book *Wearingness of the Self*, the French sociologist Alain Ehrenberg drew attention to the explosive rise in depression, as well as a general state of exhaustion; even pain often represented masked depression. The numbers have skyrocketed since then. In this society we can never arrive. Instead of pride in one's work, there is talk of pride in exhaustion[9] – to emphasise in small talk that things are going well, but that we are very stressed, sometimes appears to be a sign of belonging. And yet it is already true for all labour: If our time is taken from us, our life is taken from us.

But what if you were suddenly given a day off – what would you do with it? Relax and sit on the sofa? Sleep because the nights are too short and yet you often lie awake thinking of all the things you have to do? Using that recreational device you bought but never got around to using? Meeting friends – or don't they have time either? Finally clean the flat properly, something you've wanted to do for a long time? Or does an extra day mean just one more day when you don't know what to do with your time? The flat is cleaned, and if not – who can see that, anyway? Leaving the flat is hardly possible without a compulsion to consume. So how to go out when money is tight? If money is no problem, however, everything that is missing is quickly procured – why go to the shopping mall, after all? And sitting in bars and cafés soon becomes stodgy.

Yet, everyone enjoys doing something – unless they are depressed. But even young people lack the time and opportunities to discover their desire for a variety of activities. We live in a society that not only denies most of us the possibility to consume, but also the opportunity to do something meaningful. To be able to devote ourselves to what we consider really important would mean, to use Karl Marx's words, to realise our true being.

Labour can make us feel useful and it often feels better than sitting at home in front of a screen. But labour does not mean self-determination. We have to work in alienated conditions. Alienation can mean, as an animal-loving person having to slaughter pigs in order to be able to pay food and rent – that is, a job we don't identify with. But even if we can turn our hobby into a job, that means, to put it blunty, having to go for a walk in the forest every Monday morning until the afternoon, Monday to Friday, and preferably for the rest of our lives and always doing this better than the others who also want this great job. Or to put it another way: As workers we might stand on the assembly line, as managers we fly through the world with all our soft skills. But in both cases, the requirement of adding (surplus) value does not really leave room for individual development. This does not even change fundamentally with self-employment; then, also, even a hobby that has become a profession must be geared to market pressures. Individual features are only appreciated and tolerated insofar as they can be transformed into monetary value.

It was not with deconstructivism that the term "alienation" became problematic; Marx had already switched to "reification" in order not to suggest that there was an underlying unalienated true human nature. But understanding that we are always part of our society, that we as individuals would develop quite differently in a different historical situation, does not mean that human beings are absorbed in every circumstance of life without suffering – otherwise the approach described in Aldous Huxley's dystopian novel *Brave New World* (1932) of conditioning embryos in artificial wombs already for their future profession (and class) would be convincingly possible. There is no natural state of the human being independent of society, but we are more than its imprints.

Not being able to start from a natural "so-ness" of the human being makes it difficult to grasp non-alienation. Hartmut Rosa's concept of "resonance" thus convincingly fills a gap. Yet resonance is not to be equated with self-determination in the sense of autonomy. Being in love is a moment of most intense resonance but it is not an autonomous state and it is a very vulnerable one. Resonance also does not merge with meaningfulness – walking in the forest can be a very intense experience full of resonance, but it does not particularly make sense. Resonances are moments of transformation through touch, but at the same time more than the addition of moments, namely a form of relating to the world, of articulating, of transformation. Rosa repeatedly refers to Herbert Marcuse and his design of an "erotic", "libidinous" relation to life as a whole, not understood individually, but as a societal alternative (Rosa 2016:41).

In contrast, according to Rosa, every fear is a resonance killer, because it prevents people from opening up and becoming, and tends to make them incapable of encountering each other. The basic relationship between people in the market economy is one of competition and fear, often disguised as other fears, behind which is nothing other than the fear of failing, of not being enough. Which leads to the next reason why a good life for all is not possible with a market economy: The pressure to exploit generates structural hatred.

If in the apple–banana example, or more precisely the one with no apple but a pile of bananas, my competitor can massage better than I can, and therefore gets the bananas I need in order not to suffer hardship, this rarely happens without negative feelings. But even if we don't feel them, we still have to behave as if we hate the others. If we write a CV that shows how many massage internships we have done, we are trying nothing other than to make everyone else's CV inferior to ours.

Having to understand each other as competitors means structural hatred as the basis of our competitive society. Especially since the defeats in the competition of a society of exploitation cannot be put away with the solidity of a good loser as Eva von Redecker puts it: Not only whether one can afford the trendy salad, but whether one has a home at all depends on one's own market value (2020:14). To this I would add: It's about much more than that. It is about recognition, about our self-worth, about the feeling of being needed.

Market logic always means structural hatred, because it means having to live and do business against each other and not with each other. Thus it becomes clear what Gerrard Winstanley meant in the mid-17th century when he declared that it makes no difference whether one lives among enemies or brothers, as long as one works for a wage. He was a leading figure of the Diggers, the movement in England that sought to reclaim land as commons and saw property and the system of buying and selling as the root of all evil.

Notes

1 This and the following quotation are taken from https://www.marxists.org/archive/marx/works/1867-c1/ch06.htm
2 See https://womin.africa (15.06.2023).
3 See https://www.spiegel.de/ausland/grossbritannien-verbaende-warnen-vor-lage-in-notaufnahmen-a-6cb74e2c-8f28-4f93-885c-d2c037442dde (02.01.2023, last accessed 15.06.2023).
4 Maria Mast/Fabian Herringer (2019) “Die Menschen betteln, um auf Toilette gehen zu dürfen”, in: *Die Zeit* 25.11.2019; https://www.zeit.de/arbeit/2019-11/altenpflege-pflegeheim-menschenwuerde-beruf-fachkraeftemangel (15.06.2023).
5 See e.g. European Environmental Bureau (2019) “Decoupling Debunked. Evidence and Arguments against Green Growth as a Sole Strategy for Sustainability”, https://eeb.org/library/decoupling-debunked/(15.06.2023).
6 Raj Patel, “The History of the World in 7 Cheap Things”; https://www.youtube.com/watch?v=BAJgGFtF44A, min. 14 (15.06.2023).
7 Christian Stöcker (2021): “Exponentielles Covid-Wachstum: Die Zukunft kommt schneller, als Sie denken”, Spiegel-online column 04.10.2021; https://www.spiegel.de/wissenschaft/mensch/exponentielles-corona-wachstum-die-zukunft-kommt-schneller-als-sie-denken-kolumne-a-121911ce-1638-4698-ad9a-28a7f3443d98 (15.06.2023).
8 Westphalen (2022) speaks of 128 studies that already proved this connection at the turn of the millennium: Westphalen, Alexander von (2022) Altruismus – Der Mensch in Zeiten der Katastrophe; https://share.deutschlandradio.de/dlf-audiothek-audio-teilen.html?audio_id=dira_DLF_a2f60714 (15.06.2023).
9 According to psychologist Stephan Grünewald: https://www.manager-magazin.de/harvard/fuehrung/stephan-gruenewald-erschoepfungsstolz-durch-werkstolz-ersetzen-a-00000000-0002-0001-0000-000172382636 (08.06.2023).

References

Davis, Mike (2000) *Late Victorian Holocaust. El Niño Famines and the Making of the Third World*, London/New York: Verso.

Duhm, Dieter (1972) *Angst im Kapitalismus. Zweiter Versuch der gesellschaftlichen Begründung zwischenmenschlicher Angst in der kapitalistischen Warengesellschaft*, Lampertheim: Verlag Kübler KG, 1976.

Graeber, David (2011) *Debt. The First 5000 Years*, New York: Melville House; quoted from *Schulden. Die ersten 5000 Jahre*, Stuttgart: Klett-Cotta, 2012.

Ehrenberg, Alain (1998) *Das erschöpfte Selbst. Depression und Gesellschaft in der Gegenwart*, Frankfurt M./: dtv, 2008.

Hartmann, Evi (2016) *Wie viele Sklaven halten Sie? Über Globalisierung und Moral*, Frankfurt M./New York: Campus.

Hartsock, Nancy M. (1983) *Money, Sex, and Power. Toward a Feminist Historical Materialism*, Boston: Northeastern University Press.

Haug, Frigga (1996) *Frauen-Politiken*, Berlin: Argument.

Hochschild, Arlie Russell (2000) "Global Care Chains and Emotional Surplus Value", in W. Hutton/A. Giddens (eds) *On The Edge. Living with Global Capitalism*, London: Jonathan Cape.

Lessenich, Stephan (2016) *Neben uns die Sintflut. Die Externalisierungsgesellschaft und ihr Preis*, Berlin: Carl Hanser Verlag; translated as *Living Well at Other's Expense. The Hidden Costs of Western Prosperity*, Medford: Polity Press, 2019.

Luxemburg, Rosa (1913) *Die Akkumulation des Kapitals. Ein Beitrag zur ökonomischen Erklärung des Imperialismus*, Frankfurt: Verlag Neue Kritik, 1966.

Moore, Jason W. (2015a) *Capitalism in the Web of Life. Ecology and the Accumulation of Capital*, London/New York: Verso; *translated into German as Kapitalismus im Lebensnetz. Ökologie und die Akkumulation des Kapitals*, Berlin: Matthes & Seitz, 2020.

Moore, Jason W. (2015b) "Endless Accumulation, Endless (Unpaid) Work?", in: *Occupied Times*; http://theoccupiedtimes.org/?p=13766 (15. 06. 2023).

Müller, Beatrice (2016) *Wert-Abjektion. Abwertung von Care-Arbeit im patriarchalen Kapitalismus am Beispiel der ambulanten Pflege*, Münster: Westfälisches Dampfboot.

Neusüß, Christel (1985) *Die Kopfgeburten der Arbeiterbewegung oder Die Genossin Luxemburg bringt alles durcheinander*, Hamburg/Zürich: Rasch&Röhring.

Nixon, Rob (2011) *Slow Violence and the Environmentalism of the Poor*, Cambridge, MA: Harvard.

Patel, Raj/Moore, Jason W. (2017) *A History of the World in Seven Cheap Things. A Guide to Capitalism, Nature, and the Future of the Planet*, Oakland: University of California Press.

Pfeffer, Jeffrey/Sutton, Robert I. (2000) *The Knowing-doing Gap. How Smart Companies Turn Knowledge into Action*, Boston: Harvard Business Press.

Prebisch, Raul (1950) *The Economic Development of Latin America and its Principal Problems*, New York: United Nations.

Rosa, Hartmut (2016) *Resonanz. Eine Soziologie der Weltbeziehung*, Frankfurt/M.: Suhrkamp.

Redecker, Eva von (2020) *Revolution für das Leben. Philosophie der neuen Protestformen*, Frankfurt/M.: S.Fischer.

Santarius, Tilman (2012) "Grünes Wachstum. Der Mythos ist eine Milchmädchenrechnung", *Zeitschrift politische Ökologie* 130, 132–135.

Schlaudt, Oliver (2023) "The Market as a 'Rigged Game'. Theories of Ecologically Unequal Exchange and their Implications for Value, Price, and Measures of Real Wealth", in: Isabel Feichtner/Geoff Gordon (eds), *Constitutions of Value. Law, Governance, and Economic Value*, New York: Routledge, 276–294.

Smith, Adam (1776) *An Inquiry into the Nature and Causes of the Wealth of Nations*, London: Strahan&Cadell; quoted from *Wohlstand der Nationen*, München: dtv, 1990.

Spivak, Gayatri Chakravorty (1988) *A Critique of Postcolonial Reason. Toward a History of the Vanishing Present*, Cambridge/London: Harvard University Press.

Varoufakis, Yanis (2013) *Talking to my Daughter. A Brief History of Capitalism*, London: Penguin Random House.

5

OVER*COMMONING* CAPITALISM

Can there be a way out of exploitation and externalisation that does justice to the theoretical and economic intersectional analysis? And how do we finally get out of the trash compactor whose walls – symbolising climate and other crises – are coming ever closer?

In the ecofeminist analysis of the 1980s and 1990s, to enlarge the subsistence was largely considered the solution. In the beginning, the accusation of romanticising, of glossing over the conditions in the part of the iceberg under water, which are anything but freely designed, was not entirely unjustified. This led to the explicit call for the politicisation of subsistence and "dissident subsistence".

It is not about a "side-by-side" of subsistence and market economy in the sense of perpetual co-existence. Or more precisely: it is not about maintaining the spheres above and below the surface of the water, nor about maintaining an inside in the hegemonic bloc and an outside. Instead, it is about dissolving the boundaries that form the triangles and squares of externalisation and thus exploitation. Emancipation is impossible without structural dissolution of subject positions. As long as money and the market are adhered to, neither the exploitation of the externalised nor the anti-emancipatory effects, such as alienation, structural hatred or unjust distribution effects, even within the monetarily profiting areas, will be abolished.

DOI: 10.4324/9781003373360-5

There is no good market economy beyond evil capitalism: Every market has the consequences described, even if it is state-regulated (which it always has to be, anyway, in order not to collapse), even if it could function without a financial market or capital concentration (which it cannot), and is thus always exploiting and always externalising. Even if the enterprise belongs to the workers. Even if the means of production are nationalised. And in the theoretical case of an omnipotent benevolent state intending nothing but the good life for all, why should it constantly work against these effects of the market undermining emancipation instead of directly acting benevolent? However, the contradiction lies deeper, since such a state would also have to be dependent on taxes from the market economy and on repression, and thus on exploitation and externalisation.

As mentioned at the beginning of the book, Gopal Dayaneni takes the *Star Wars* heroes' attempt to stop the walls with a big metal rod as an allegory: Just as the trash compactor is there to destroy metal, solutions fail that try to fight via the market what the market has unleashed. In fact, almost all current alternatives critical of capitalism leave the logic of exchange and thus the market and money untouched – including some that this book refers to for analysis. But this leads to a theoretical break in their argumentative build-up. For to demand measures such as a reduction in working hours and/or an unconditional basic income without developing a broader perspective does not do justice to their own analysis concerning the structural results of the market. Such demands are not wrong – but as steps on the way they must lead to a form of societal reproduction that goes beyond these measures. However, property, labour and exchange are not considered fundamentally questionable by the vast majority of critics of capitalism.

To stay with Dayaneni's image: It seems understandable that we reach for the metal bar in the face of the crises. However, numerous movements from the Global South have long been articulating that, in order to solve the crises, the market logic as their main cause must be overcome. The fact that this is so little known is largely due to what Spivak analysed as "the subaltern cannot speak".

I personally had the honour to serve as press coordinator for Peoples' Global Action (PGA), a network of grassroots movements from pretty much all over the world. PGA grew out of the global networking initiated by the Zapatistas in the mid-1990s, united by hallmarks, in particular: "the very clear rejection of capitalism" as well as "all forms of and systems of domination and discrimination", "a call for direct action" and "an organisational philosophy based on decentralisation and autonomy".[1] It was PGA who Sbegan the protests against the World Trade Organization in 1998 and hence the alterglobalisation movement – in *Geschichte wird gemacht* (Habermann 2014) I provide a kind of personal historiography of this movement. It was in this context that I got to know commons – and it took me a decade to understand them.

Admittedly, it was the time when mainstream academia also began to take an interest in the commons. Not coincidentally a year after the financial crisis, Elinor Ostrom became the first woman to win the so-called Nobel Prize in Economics in 2009 for her study of existing commons. Until then, the doctrine had prevailed that every commons would necessarily be overused as a result of anyone's individual drive for more and more. Garret Hardin, whose short 1968 article "Tragedy of the Commons" was the basis for this, had written: "Therein is the tragedy. Each man is locked into a system that compels him to increase his herd without limit – in a world that is limited" (1968:1244). But it is not the commons that compels the farmers to increase. Needs, e.g. regarding wool, can be satisfied. It is the market that compels growth without limit. Therefore we should rather speak of the *tragedy of the commodity.*

Ostrom analysed and determined eight principles which she thought to find in functioning commons. Or rather in what is called Common Pool Resources (CPR), which in mainstream economics are understood to be large resources or resource systems that are difficult to manage in a purely market-based economy because they can hardly be divided into small pieces of property. Ostrom begins her Design Principles with "Clearly defined boundaries", both of the "individuals or households who have rights to withdraw resource units" … as of "the boundaries of the CPR itself" (1990:90). Each of these expressions is full of the logic of frontiers: of the individual, of household units, of rights as rights to get individual shares. In a world that has incorporated commons as ownership for at least a millennium, this is on the one hand an important defence. On the other hand, it fails to recognise the innermost character of commons. Commons are not simply owned by a group instead of an individual.

After Ostrom's death in 2012, Silke Helfrich became the world's most renowned commons researcher. Following Christopher Alexander's example for architecture, she started looking for a pattern language of commons. These are not unconditional principles, but present the core of a solution filtered out of existing commons (which within the given structures cannot be complete) for frequently occurring problems. The pattern corresponding to Ostrom's first principle is "Create Semi-Permeable Membranes" (Bollier/Helfrich 2019:130). To illustrate the difference, let me give an example from my personal experience: For 15 years, I lived in a community where the houses were as much commons as possible under current law. For the time being, I was clearly part of the group. When I finally left, I could neither sell nor rent out my rooms. New people moved in. They became part of the group because there was available space. They did not have to pay anything nor correspond to any identity category to do so. Not by coincidence, apart from homeless sites this is probably in the monetary sense the poorest and furthermore probably one of the most mixed spaces in Germany. These days, I am not just an outsider to the group. I can come and just be there, continue to enjoy its beauties and support it in dealing with its problems. The logic of the commons is beyond the binarity of inside and outside and beyond the binarity of ownership and dispossession. It is fundamentally beyond the logic of binarities.

The logic of the commons, and thus the experiences people have in the commons are queering the binaries that limit our thinking in capitalism. These are experiences beyond labour versus laziness, egoism versus altruism, freedom versus dependence. Commons are the potential that becomes visible where these logics break or never became hegemonic. Commoning is resonance, is articulation, is transforming ourselves and the material context.

In 2013 Stefano Harney and Fred Moton published *The Undercommons: Fugitive Planning & Black Study*, followed in 2021 by *All Incomplete.* They contrast the terms undercommons and commons. "The idea of the commons leads to the presumption of interpersonal relations, and therefore of the person as an independent, strategic agent. Such persons make not just commons, but states and nations, in this worldview. The undercommons is the refusal of the interpersonal, and by extension the international, upon which politics is built" (2021:122).

It is not surprising that movement spaces of decades or centuries of dissident resistance are such spaces of other logics – be they called commons or otherwise, and as incomplete as they may be – and therefore voices against the market are often raised from the margins of this world. Not only within Peoples' Global Action. Market-based and technological solutions of the UN climate negotiations were also called "false solutions" by the *Delhi Climate Justice Declaration* of 2002. Similarly, in 2009, during the UN Climate Change Conference COP in Copenhagen, representatives of grassroots movements from Asia, Africa and Latin America agreed on the message that "market based solutions […] lead to 'climate colonialism'". And in Paris in 2015, despite the ban on demonstrations, indigenous peoples from different parts of the world formed red lines symbolising that even adherence to the targeted solutions would continue to destroy their livelihoods. They criticised that through the pricing of CO_2 and nature in general, the co-environment is being degraded to a commodity.[2]

But in reproducing indigenous positions, I can hardly escape the dangers of homogenisation, romanticisation or at least that of the omnipotent white eye. Instead, I want to focus on my own experiences from the German-speaking area, without wanting to imply that other places in the world are less suitable.

In 2020, the *Network Economic Transformation* (Netzwerk Oekonomischer Wandel – NOW) was founded. Silke Helfrich represented the commons movement, others did so for degrowth, solidarian economy or other approaches; including myself for an exchange logic free Ecommony. NOW was based on the experience of an earlier networking, called Nürnberg Netz, which reminded me of TAMARA as the answer to Margret Thatcher's "There is no alternative", which has gone down in history as the TINA principle. TAMARA stood for "There Are Many And Realistic Alternatives". To me, this always sounded like single individuals isolated at desks thinking up alternatives and then discussing them with or, very often, against each other. But with NOW, those of us who represented a movement joined together and proclaimed: "We have come together to represent in diversity what unites us – the understanding that our different paths lead to a common vision: a deeply democratic and needs-based society."[3] After Silke Helfrich's fatal accident in the mountains of Liechtenstein in 2021, and in order to open up for activists from a variety of social movements, we relaunched and became NOW NET (including the English abbreviation). In this new formulation, the three paths that have become evident for this transformation are:

dismantling the market
democratising the society comprehensively
creating commons.[4]

Dismantling the market by reducing mechanisms of competition

Understanding that the market and thus the logic of profit and competition is neither a law of nature nor a necessity shows the possibility of overcoming it. Aligning the economy with the common good and thus reducing market competition in order to dismantle the market is the most far-reaching starting point for transformation from the perspective of NOW NET and one of the three paths.

The first steps in this direction can be taken in many ways. One movement whose founder Christian Felber co-initiated NOW is the *Economy for the Common Good* (ECG). The ECG has developed the Common Good Balance Sheet. With this tool, the ECG provides a point system with which companies (and other organisations) can check to what extent their working conditions, supply chain, etc. comply with values such as human dignity, ecological sustainability, social justice, and democratic co-determination. In this way, their actual production conditions ideally become visible to everybody, or at least more transparent, and this information can be used by consumers when making purchasing decisions. While more than a thousand companies in 35 countries have so far joined in voluntarily, ECG is calling for the Common Good Balance Sheet to be made mandatory. ECG also advocates that such companies with a good ranking should be given preferential treatment, for example through tax breaks, easier access to credit, or preferential treatment in public contracts.

More informed purchasing decisions are certainly not to be confused with democratic decisions. Christian Felber himself points out that in the USA the best paid manager earns 350,000 times the legal minimum wage (2012:32). But at least transparency makes decisions more democratic compared to price signals providing the only information. After all, anyone who studies marketing knows that being more expensive does not necessarily mean that labour and other standards are better observed.

The Economy for the Common Good does not seem a particularly radical step. But the ECG can also be understood as pushing back the pure market mechanism. And why should the democratic moment be limited at some point? Accordingly, in his utopia *Gemeinwohlökonomie* (*Change Everything*) (2012), Felber sees the ECG as leading to an economy in which workers decide democratically on production and the use of funds, and even the financial market is completely democratically designed. Money and financial market without monetary and financial market function, however, can simply be abolished.

A much more far-reaching form of dismantling the market are community supported businesses. The corresponding German-speaking network calls itself Community Supported Everything (CSX), the best known part of which is Community Supported Agriculture (CSA). The basic idea is that instead of price formation on the market, there is cooperation between producers and consumers (which often merges into prosumers, for example when the consumers help out on the farm). While the original model was that of a fixed membership fee in exchange for a fixed vegetable box, this has been changing on both sides in recent years. Now, a large proportion of the nearly 500 CSAs in Germany practice more flexible forms of withdrawal that take into account desire for and need for vegetables varying widely. And instead of a fixed monetary contribution, there is often only a guideline. In many cases, the process now runs as follows: Producers name the amount they expect to need in the following year for outside expenses, such as machinery, fuel, etc. This process is designed to be transparent. Thereupon, the consumers organise an anonymous bidding round, where everyone is completely free to name their contribution. If it is not enough, the process is repeated until it matches. Possibly non-monetary contributions reducing the required amount are taken into consideration.

But even the broad-based demands of social movements are often nothing else than proposals to reduce market competition: Redistributing wealth and guaranteeing basic material security for all; getting out of environmentally disastrous technologies and into new ones; time for change by reducing labour time; space and good conditions for care in all its aspects; and, last but not least, insisting on justice being indivisible. These seven demands have been found as the common points of almost all relevant emancipatory movements in Germany in 2020 in a networking called Plattform Solidarische Transformation. These are reformist steps. But radical protests also contain demands (otherwise they would be rebellions) – for instance to abolish the police. In capitalism such demands can at best be partially realised. For example, to defund the police (which, by the way, as Ostrom had already found out in the 1960s, is strengthening the community and thus reducing crime). Wherever successes can be achieved, they open up scope for transformative action. But even demands that are not realistic within the given conditions serve to shift the common sense in such a way that the reproduction of the structures might no longer be supported by a critical mass.

To give an example for this shifting: The Berlin-based initiative *Deutsche Wohnen & Co Enteignen* [DWE – Expropriate Deutsche Wohnen & Co]advocates expropriating the portfolios of companies with more than 3,000 flats. Just a few years ago, expropriation seemed beyond common sense. After a campaign supported by many activists, about 60 per cent of the votes were in favour of expropriation in the 2021 Berlin referendum.

The first of the paths advocated by NOW NET thus allows two currents to converge that would normally seem irreconcilable. First, demands for reform. This is not reduced to verbal forms. Butler also draws attention to this by referring to the expression “Put your body on the line”. This could be the police line, the crossing of which is threatened by sanctions. But even more generally, “lives make claims in all sorts of ways” (Butler 2000:178). On the other hand, using Direct Action, understood as anticipating the desired state (Graeber 2009), to organise with less market or already beyond the market, as far as it is possible within the existing structures. These two paths go together even better, because arguments about whether the market ultimately needs to be abolished are not necessary as long as it is always clear that structures must not conflict with truly democratic will. So people could decide this later (spoiler: yes, the market does always conflict with democracy…). Which brings us to the second way, which runs parallel and yet leads much further. Or to put it a little differently: To dismantle the market is the starting point, democracy is the compass.

Democratising democracy

If it is no longer the market that distributes resources, then these decisions must be made differently. If we do not trust in any kind of centralised state (history advises us not to), then society needs to be democratised. But what does that mean? In his book *Crack Capitalism* (2010), John Holloway also chooses a trash compactor as an image, only he doesn’t call the room by that name. And it is furnished, reminiscent of the image of the house in chapter 2, symbolising the structures that limit us, which we, it is recalled, can also dismantle and reconstruct.

> People do not seem to see the walls advancing. From time to time there are elections about how to place the furniture. These elections are not unimportant: they make some people more comfortable, others less so, they may even affect the speed at which the walls are moving, but they do nothing to stop their relentless advance.
>
> *(2010:8)*

Just like this picture, the daily news, to which Bini Adamczak refers in the opening quote to chapter 1, obviously shows that this form of electoral democracy does not contribute anything to averting the impending destruction. This form of democracy is part of the nation state, historically based on property, exploitation and externalisation. It cannot overcome what it is based on. Real democracy is more than going to the polls. Real democracy means all people having a say in all decisions affecting them. In all areas of society. And real democracy does not mean the hegemony of the majority, but – to use one of the patterns of commoning – to bring diversity into shared purpose. Clearly, there is a lack of historical experience for truly democratic conditions without any exclusions. Yet many movements are already developing new ways for this, and numerous methods already exist.

Initiatives to push back the market already go hand in hand with more democracy. As with CSX, where decisions are made collectively and different interests are taken into account. As with DWE. Societalisation is not nationalisation, it is neither state nor market, "there is democracy in it", they say.[5] DWE put a concrete proposal on the table about how the 243,000 societalised flats should be managed in the public sector in the future. The proposal contains differentiated concepts, including fair housing allocation, climate protection and democratic co-determination of tenants. The proposed model of an institution under public law is the closest you can come under current German law towards a Commons Public Partnership, where the state provides most material resources, but the people decide.

Not surprisingly, such approaches always wrestle with the legal logic of property, since property is considered the starting point of the legal system, and historically, legal fictions have served to destroy the commons. There are a few lawyers who devote themselves to finding legal forms for such approaches so that they can be integrated into the existing legal system, as well as to designing alternative legal models. As limited as this can be within the existing system, this struggle can be a step along the way and broaden the horizon.

For Harney and Moton, John Locke does not only represent the legitimisation of property and the legal system based on it, but he also stands for a subject constitution, "beginning with the positing/positioning of a body for locating ownership, and the owned, and a mind for owning" thus creating "the tabula rasa as a container for properties – properties of the mind, and properties owned by the propertied mind". This space, it does not only contain our bodies, but also our minds. "From the first moment, which appears to keep happening all the time, all property is posited, beginning with the positing/positioning of a body for locating ownership, and the owned, and a mind for owning" (2021:14).

This is reminiscent of how Foucault conceives the state: as a technique of control, as a dynamic form and historical fixation of societal power relations. Identities are also tied to the state, and Foucault describes it as a central political goal to free ourselves from both the state and the type of individualisation associated with it. We would have to bring about new forms of subjectivity by rejecting the type of individuality that has been imposed on us. We have to extend our thinking and build what we can in order to shake off this type of political "double-bind" that consists in simultaneous individualisation and totalisation through modern power structures (Foucault 1982:250).

Derrida distinguishes between the exercise of law, legalised and legitimised by a regulated system of laws, and a justice that must always be re-established as a relationship to the other. The exercise of law must always refer to past formulations of justice, but since in the encounter with the other the same no longer remains the same and the relationship to the other does not close, every decision represents a singularity. In this way, democracy is always in the making. Derrida therefore speaks of *démocratie à venir*, of democracy to come (Derrida 1992).

His related concept of the "double gesture" brings the identity categories back into focus. The first gesture is to overturn the hierarchy. The second gesture of deconstruction is to dissolve the underlying binary logic so that new concepts emerge. To illustrate: Patriarchy says men are rational and women are emotional, and being rational is better, so the second wave of feminism responded by saying being emotional is better. The third wave of feminism began to sublate this binarity, and many possibilities of being became visible. This is what queering is about.

In this book, there is often talk of a "we". But who are "we"? All those who are interested in transformation, says Adamczak.[6] This means avoiding exclusions based on identity categories here too, along the lines of "You are a landlord, you may not", "You are white and male, you may not". It is not how we were constructed that counts, but how we become. But this must not be confused with indeterminacy. Unlearning privilege remains central. Our top of the house residents could learn not to be happy there; at least that is what empirical studies show (Pickett/Wilkenson 2010). Just as nowadays hardly anyone dreams of becoming a slave owner. And yet: People in privileged positions rarely give up their privileges voluntarily. Their horizons cannot yet grasp that privileges are poisoned (as Spivak has made us aware). And this brings us to the problem Stephan Lessenich describes with the term externalisation society and the limits of its democracy: Why should a privileged society abolish its own privileges if the subalterns are not even in the same discourse space?

The first gesture of deconstruction, of emancipation, of overthrowing the hierarchy, could of course be the classic revolution. But that would not be sufficient for a fully emancipatory society without the second gesture of overcoming the underlying logic. First, because a dictatorship of the working class is obviously not a society free of domination. Second, it might solve classism but in the identity of a working class one cannot overcome market society and its discontents. Just as Marx wrote in the *Economic and Philosophical Manuscripts of 1944*: Even equality of wages would only transform society into an abstract capitalist. Thirdly, as many revolutions would be needed as there are antagonisms. Perhaps even of the young against the old who are willing to destroy the climate. Of course, reality is much more fuzzy, but this is ultimately the case with any relation of power.

John Holloway reminds us that Marx's

> understanding of capitalism was based not on the antagonism between two groups of people but on the antagonism in the way in which human social practice is organised […] The social antagonism is thus not in the first place a conflict between two groups of people […] rather it is a conflict about the subordination of social practice, about the fetishisation of social relations.
>
> *(2002:146f)*

The transformative "we" is not an all-encompassing we, but a situated we, a "we" in the making. It helps to realise that we all cannot remain what we are. Someone built this house, many people did, and we ourselves are always caught contributing to its maintenance.

And what about the chickens – are they interested in transformation? I would say: Yes, certainly! Yet, Spivak, and Butler with Spivak, rightly point out that the attempt of translation, i.e. to "let subalterns speak", always bears the risk of appropriation. Instead, a language between languages has to be found.

> Indeed, the task will be not to assimilate the unspeakable into the domain of speakability in order to house it there, within the existing norms of dominance, but to shatter the confidence of dominance, to show how equivocal its claims to universality are, and, from that equivocation, track the break-up of its regie, an opening towards alternative versions of universality.
>
> *(Butler 2000:179)*

Why should this not apply for all in the web of life? It is worth recalling that in Western thought being human was in doubt in the 16th century in relation to indigenous people and in the 17th to women.

Was it only economic developments and/or violent upheavals that made changes in past forms of domination possible, or does something also play a role that Harney/Moton summarise as "hapticality, the capacity to feel through others, for others to feel through you, for you to feel them feeling" (2021:98)? What happens to human and more-than-human animals when, through a more than passive grasping (this is what haptic stands for, following the psychologist Max Dessoir), the non-speaking impediment of one is no longer taken for granted by the other? No human language is needed to express not wanting to be destined as chicken nuggets. This is not about the self-experiment of a human whether they can live with a chicken for some time and kill it without any need. If our mind is a container for properties, to put it with Harney/Moton, we can. Slave owners also lived with the enslaved. Again the scene in Dostoyevsky's *Crime and Punishment* comes to mind, in which someone beats his horse to death in agony with the words "It's my property, I'll do what I choose". But what happens, when we open more than passively to letting the frontier of hyperseparation become more permeable?

In an ecofeminist-inspired book by the group Schwertfisch from 1997, Hans-Jürgen Stolz writes that life is the most hated concept in left discourse.

> It is understandable that the left must be afraid of relativising man, who has been knocked off his high pedestal as the 'crown of creation': If everything non-human is regarded as a mere resource that can be used at will, then 'relativised man' is also threatened with this fate. On the other hand, anyone who really starts from the unity of nature as the point of reference for liberation does not extend the Enlightenment contempt for non-human life to the human being.
>
> *(Schwertfisch 1997:188)*

No, the reverse of this cannot be thought in the prevailing logics. What might emerge if it is the whole web of life with which we can articulate ourselves in resonance and reconstruct our world?

Hapticality as a feeling of the shipped, where to "feel others is unmediated, immediately social, among us" (Harney/Moton 2021:98) is a feeling that occurs more easily in the crowded margins, but also in the cracks that John Holloway sees in the walls, where the angular logics of property and equivalent exchange do not fit. Those who can only see as far as the limits of their property and take those to be the limits of their happiness cannot understand when Harney/Moton write: "They like being incomplete", adding with reference to Paolo Freire "the more we think of ourselves as complete, finished, whole, individual, the more we cannot love or be loved" (2021:41). Perhaps this is the semi-permeable membrane of the transformative "we": Whoever is able to feel for others through themselves, for themselves, to feel them as they feel you, this feeling which overflows every state and every container for identity, is "we". That, too, can only ever be a situated "we". To become a critical mass for transformation, we may have to liberate – in cracks, in spaces of other logics, in (under)commons – this

> feel you want more of, which releases you. The closest Marx ever got to the general antagonism was when he said 'from each according to his ability, to each according to his need' but we have read this as the possession of ability and the possession of need. What if we thought of the experiment of the hold as the absolute fluidity, the informality, of this condition of need and ability? What if ability and need were in constant play and we found someone who dispossessed us so that this movement was our inheritance. Your love makes me strong, your love makes me weak.
>
> *(Harney/Moton 2013:99)*

Quoting this, I resist the urge to omit this last sentence, recalling a talk by an indigenous representative who, on a panel at a climate camp on the North Sea coast in 2021, in the midst of a blockade of a coal freighter carried out in small boats, said that after centuries of resistance they had come to the conclusion that only love can save us. The German interpreter translated that we should take care of each other. As far as I could tell, what was lost in this is an element that is overflowing hegemonic left discourse.

Harney/Moton also describe hapticality as "the feel that what is to come is here" (2021:98). Adamczak emphasises the importance of starting here and now with other ways of relating instead of focusing on a revolution. But she also says: We can theoretically say goodbye to revolutions – they will still come. And yes, Adamczak says, it takes the fierceness and speed of the revolutionary movement, to get out of the structures and rebuild them. But to focus on this very quickly constructs an "us" versus "them". And any binary logic will turn power-with into power-over. In contrast, democratic articulation implies changing identities. Changing identities imply changing the societal context, which cannot be thought of independently. Power-with could become a becoming-with. This makes the impossible the horizon.

Holloway's answer to what we can do about the approaching walls of the waste compressor: "*Break the walls*: Open the enclosed. The world of abstract labour is a world of enclosure, a world of physical and metaphorical walls. These are the encroaching walls" (2010:260). But for him, too, breaking the walls starts with cracks in the wall. These occur where we escape the dominant logics. "Start from richness", Holloway continues later, which he contrasts to monetary wealth. "Start not from your enclosure but from your force that can break that enclosure: our richness [...] our active potentialities, our absolute movement of becoming" (2022:6). Listening to our own queer desires and to those of others – being more than a worker, being more than a sex object, more than chicken nuggets. We all are not fitting into the container of being interchangeable.

Creating commons

Commons arise where people act out of inner motivation and treat each other as equals. People do something not out of the compulsion to have to earn money, not because someone told them to, but because they feel a need to do it. Those who follow the compass of real democracy will reach commons, for commoning is real democracy in action. This way, we could reach a world in which many worlds fit, as the Zapatistas envisoned with their uprising in the southeast of Mexico in 1994. Because commons precisely do not prescribe a certain way of living, as the market does. Nevertheless, some essential elements form the basis of the commons. A world in which all can live in dignity, as the above quote continues, is one. Living with dignity means not being forced. The other essential element can be found in the Zapatista saying "*Todo para todos, nada para nosotros* – Everything for everyone, nothing for us" (cf. REDaktion 1997:113). It took me a long way to understand this, wondering why they did not ask for their share. But no, it is about rejecting the modern *Eigentum*, ownership, which allows us to exclude and to destroy while others suffer.

We live in democratic conditions – in other words: free – only in a society that does not force us to do anything against our own inner motivation, even economically. Inner motivation is neither to be confused with self-interest nor with fun in the matter; it can also be the insight into the necessity that becomes a need for oneself. Also, an economy or rather a mode of living is only as free as it is not at the expense of others in the web of life. Therefore, only real democracy allows for real freedom. In other words: "Only mutually can we enable us to be free." This is how NOW NET, the Network Economic Transformation puts it. Johannes Euler from the German based Commons-Institut writes: "Commons are seen as an enabling form and potential foundation for a decentralised and needs-oriented post-capitalist society free of personal and structural domination and beyond the market and state" (2016).

In the current society, taking care of needs is often prevented by market constraints. The conditions for doing so have to be built up along the way. As a result, the prevailing conditions are being dismantled simultaneously. This will not be a conflict-free path, but at the same time this might bring forth something new. The Zapatistas revolted originally against the privatisation of their land commons, and developed within a very short time practices of resistance that led to them being called the first revolution of the 21st century.[7] It is the Zapatista rebellion that begins what Marina Sitrin calls "Prefigurative Societies in Movement" (2022). But this too was based on the many years of other logics already being lived within their movement.

Re/productive practices that are not based on the exploitation of other people's labour but on commoning have to be rediscovered to a large extent. But numerous methods already exist, and in the diversity of struggles new ways are developing, being adapted to today's conditions. Commons emerge in many movements around the world, whether fighting against patents on genes, against the copyright regime or the destruction of forests. This means that any of these movements has many allies.[8]

On the website *waswirtunkoennen.jetzt* (which translates as *whatwecando.now*), NOW NET brings together a variety of steps on the three paths to dismantle the market, to democratise democracy and to create commons. As a matrix, they are organised on the one side according to what could be done individually, locally, regionally and supraregionally. On the other side, they are divided into twelve areas of life: care, food, mobility etc. Each area can be clicked on, and then on to the individual practices. Here is shared what it took to implement this practice, how to participate, and a contact is given to help transfer the project into one's own circumstances.

NOW NET is also part of the Global Tapestry of Alternatives, in which similar approaches across continents are brought into articulation.[9] Thus, they can multiply as sets of practices, each reborn as new commons, new cracks, and new ways of being-in-the-world. This does not only imply a change of the economic way of re/production, but of all power relations. Such compilations help to realise that we are at very different places on these paths, and yet on the path of overcommoning capitalism and towards the good life for all: be it in very small cracks that we can inflict on the hard structures of our daily lives, be it in a forest occupation that is maintained for years, in which people build a space of commons logic.

NOW NET is not a vibrant network – its activists are merged into their own struggles. Neither will everyone within the represented movements agree on the ways or the goal of a commons based and commons creating society beyond borders. But NOW NET's core idea that those of us who are in favour can align ourselves with the goal of a truly democratic and truly needs-based, that is, a truly emancipatory society, can become a powerful transformational force. Following these resulting interlocking ways of transformation already allows for a better life in the here and now, even though they are no smooth ways. But ruptures, be they crisis or rebellions, cannot be planned. We should not delay exploring new horizons as best we can.

David Bollier and Silke Helfrich write in their preface of *Free, Fair & Alive*:

> Those who see the inspiring activities we present in this book as painfully tiny in the face of climate change and global social dislocation fail to see not only that it is not about the scope – let alone the size – of individual projects, but about their core: about what makes them special and what can unleash their transformative power. Those who fail to see this also fail to realize what happens when a seed sprouts. This is like looking at a grain of rice, wheat, corn, potato, or bean and asking it, "But aren't you far too puny to feed humanity?"
>
> *(2019:11f)*

Commons are the potential that not only lives on, hidden under the water, but can form cracks in capitalism everywhere. When the ice melts, we become the water that breaks the walls.

Notes

1 https://www.nadir.org/nadir/initiativ/agp/free/pga/hallm.htm (15.06.2023).
2 I took part in the protests in 2009 and 2015.
3 https://netzwerk-oekonomischer-wandel.org (15.06.2023).
4 https://now-net.org (15.06.2023).
5 Vergesellschaftungskonferenz DWE Aftermovie: https://www.youtube.com/watch?v=YFnON_xun9k (15.06.2023).
6 Online-panel *Auf der Suche nach einer Utopie in der realen Transformation*, Evangelische Akademie Bad Boll, 19.02.2022.
7 *Frankfurter Rundschau*, 11.05.1994.
8 Cf. the comment by Jan Ulrich Hasek to Max Haiven: "Politik der Teilhabe (1). Haben wir ein Recht auf ein Recht auf Gemeinschaftseigentum?"; https://berlinergazette.de/recht-auf-gemeinschaftseigentum (15.06.2023).
9 https://globaltapestryofalternatives.org/ (15.06.2023).

References

Bollier, David/Helfrich, Silke (2019) *Free, Fair & Alive. The Insurgent Power of the Commons*, Gabriola: New Society Press.

Butler, Judith (2000) "Competing Universalities", in: Judith Butler/Ernesto Laclau/Slavoj Žižek: *Contingency, Hegemony, Universality. Contemporary Dialogues on the Left*, London/New York: Verso, 136–181.

Derrida, Jacques (1992) *Das andere Kap. Die vertagte Demokratie. Zwei Essays zu Europa*, Frankfurt/M.: Suhrkamp.

Euler, Johannes (2016) “Commons-creating Society. On the Radical German Commons Discourse”, *Review of Radical Political Economics*, 48(1), 93–110.

Felber, Christian (2012) *Gemeinwohlökonomie. Eine demokratische Antwort wächst*, Vienna: Deuticke/Paul Zsolnay (extended reprint), translated as *Change Everything. Creating an Economy for the Common Good*, London: Zed Books, 2015.

Foucault, Michel (1982) “Warum ich Macht untersuche: Die Frage des Subjekts”, in: Hubert L. Dreyfus/Paul Rabinow (eds.), *Michel Foucault. Jenseits von Strukturalismus und Hermeneutik*, Frankfurt: Athenäum1987, 243–250.

Graeber, David(2009) *Direct Action. An Ethnography*, Oakland/Edinburgh:AK Press.

Habermann, Friederike (2014) *Geschichte wird gemacht. Etappen des Globalen Widerstands*, Hamburg: Laika.

Harney, Stefano/Moton, Fred (2013) *The Undercommons. Fugitive Planning and Black Study*, Colchester/NewYork/Port Watson: Minor Compositions.

Harney, Stefano/Moton, Fred (2021) *All Incomplete*, Colchester/NewYork/Port Watson: Minor Compositions.

Holloway, John (2002) *Change the World Without Taking Power*, London: Plutopress.

Holloway, John (2010) *Crack Capitalism*, London: Plutopress.

Holloway, John (2022) *Hope in Hopeless Times*, London/Las Vegas: Pluto Press.

Ostrom, Elinor (1990) *Governing the Commons. The Evolution of Institutions for Collective Action*, Cambridge: Cambrige University Press.

Pickett, Kate/Wilkenson, Richard (2010) *The Spirit Level. Why Equality is Better for Everyone*, New York: Bloomsbury Press.

REDaktion (1997) *Chiapas und die Internationale der Hoffnung*, Köln: isp.

Redecker, Eva von (2020) *Revolution für das Leben. Philosophie der neuen Protestformen*, Frankfurt/M.: S.Fischer.

Schwertfisch (1997) *Zeitgeist mit Gräten. Politische Perspektiven zwischen Ökologie und Autonomie*, Bremen: Yetipress.

Sitrin, Marina (2022) “Prefigurative Societies in Movement, in: https://globaltapestryofalternatives.org/newsletters:09:collaboration (15.06.2023).

INDEX

For Product Safety Concerns and Information please contact our EU representative GPSR@taylorandfrancis.com
Taylor & Francis Verlag GmbH, Kaufingerstraße 24, 80331 München, Germany

www.ingramcontent.com/pod-product-compliance
Ingram Content Group UK Ltd.
Pitfield, Milton Keynes, MK11 3LW, UK
UKHW022157190926
475702UK00003B/72
9781032446806